DO YOU SPEAK GOLF?

International Golfers'
Language Guide

for

WESTERN EUROPE
NORTH, CENTRAL, and
SOUTH AMERICA

ENGLISH
to
Norwegian
Swedish
Danish
Dutch
German
French
Italian
Spanish
Portuguese

by

D0580701

First printing
Printed in the USA

Pandemic International Publishers Inc.
POB 61849
Vancouver, Washington 98666
(U.S.A.)

TABLE OF CONTENTS

SECTIONS COVERED IN EACH LANGUAGE

Basic conversation
At the golf course
Paying
Renting
Golf equipment
Clubs
Golf terms
At the pro-shop
Colours
Numbers

"Monsieur Rene, Herr Schmitt, I am your
instructor for today"

PREFACE

This practical guide is intended to aid you, the international golfer, while travelling throughout Western Europe, North, Central, and South America.

The largest problem you may encounter is that phrase books for travellers do not provide translations for the specialized vocabulary used at the golf course. In preparing this book I have taken many suggestions from avid golfers who frequently travel abroad to play golf. This enabled me to compile a phrase book to help you overcome some of these barriers.

This guide is easy to use with the contents logically arranged. The English phrase or word is given followed by the foreign equivalent; with a complete phonetic transcription (shown in brackets) to enable you to pronounce every word correctly.

For example, the Spanish:

I am here: yo soy aquí (yoh soy ahkee)

DISTANCES

Inches - Centimeters		Centimeters - Inches	
1	2.54	1	0.39
2	5.08	2	0.79
3	7.62	3	1.18
4	10.16	4	1.58
5	12.70	5	1.95
6	15.24	6	2.36
7	17.78	7	2.76
8	20.32	8	3.15
9	22.86	9	3.54
10	25.40	10	3.93
11	27.94	11	4.32
12	30.48	12	4.71

Feet - Meters		Meters - Feet	
1	0.30	1	3.28
2	0.61	2	6.56
3	0.91	3	9.84
4	1.22	4	13.12
5	1.52	5	16.40
6	1.83	6	19.69
7	2.13	7	22.97
8	2.44	8	26.25
9	2.74	9	29.53
10	3.05	10	32.81

Feet - Meters		Meters - Feet	
11	3.35	11	36.09
12	3.66	12	39.37
13	3.96	13	42.63
14	4.27	14	45.93
15	4.57	15	49.21
16	4.88	16	52.50
17	5.18	17	55.78
18	5.49	18	59.06
19	5.79	19	62.34
20	6.10	20	65.62

Yards - Meters		Meters - Yards	
1	0.91	1	1.09
2	1.83	2	2.19
3	2.74	3	3.28
4	3.66	4	4.37
5	4.57	5	5.47
6	5.49	6	6.56
7	6.40	7	7.66
8	7.32	8	8.65
9	8.23	9	9.84
10	9.15	10	10.93
11	10.06	11	11.99
12	10.98	12	13.08
13	11.90	13	14.17
14	12.81	14	15.26
15	13.72	15	16.35
20	18.30	20	21.86
25	22.87	25	27.33
30	27.45	30	32.79
40	36.60	40	43.72
50	45.75	50	54.65
60	54.90	60	65.58
70	64.05	70	76.51
75	68.62	75	81.98
80	73.20	80	87.44
90	82.35	90	98.37
100	91.50	100	109.30
125	114.37	125	136.62
150	137.25	150	163.95
175	160.12	175	191.27
200	183.00	200	218.60
225	205.87	225	245.92
250	228.75	250	273.25
300	274.50	300	327.90
400	366.00	400	437.20
500	457.50	500	546.50

Miles - Kilometers		Kilometers - Miles	
1	1.61	1	0.62
2	3.22	2	1.24
3	4.83	3	1.86
4	6.44	4	2.48
5	8.05	5	3.11
6	9.66	6	3.73
7	11.27	7	4.35
8	12.88	8	4.97
9	14.49	9	5.59
10	16.10	10	6.21
20	32.20	20	12.43
30	48.28	30	18.64
40	64.37	40	24.85
50	80.47	50	31.07
100	160.93	100	62.14
200	321.90	200	124.30
500	804.70	500	310.70

SIZES
(sizes are approximate)

MEN

SHIRTS

Continental	36	37	38	39	41	42	43			
UK	14	14½	15	15½	16	16½	17			
USA	14	14½	15	15½	16	16½	17			

SHOES

Continental	34	35½	36½	38	39	41	42	43	44	45
UK	2	3	4	5	6	7	8	9	10	11
USA	3½	4½	5½	6½	7½	8½	9½	10½	11½	12½

TROUSERS

Continental	66	71	76	81	86	91	97	102	107	112
UK	26	28	30	32	34	36	38	40	42	44
USA	26	28	30	32	34	36	38	40	42	44

COATS

Continental	46	48	50	52	54	56			
UK	36	38	40	42	44	46			
USA	36	38	40	42	44	46			

HATS

Continental	54	55	56	57	58	59	60	61	62
UK	6	6	6	7	7	7½	7	7½	7
USA	6	6	7	7	7½	7	7½	7	7

SIZES
(sizes are approximate)

WOMEN

DRESSES

Continental	36	38	40	42	44	46
UK	10	12	14	16	18	20
USA	8	10	12	14	16	18

SHOES

Continental	37	38	39	41	42
UK	4	5	6	7	8
USA	6	7	8	9	10

SWEATERS

Continental	36	38	40	42	44
UK	32	34	36	38	40
USA	32	34	36	38	40

WAIST AND CHEST MEASUREMENTS

Continental	71	76	81	86	91	97	102	107	112	117
UK	28	30	32	34	36	38	40	42	44	46
USA	28	30	32	34	36	38	40	42	44	46

INTERNATIONAL GOLFERS' LANGUAGE GUIDE

NORWEGIAN

INTERNASJONALE GOLFSPILLERES SPRÅKGUIDE

NORSK

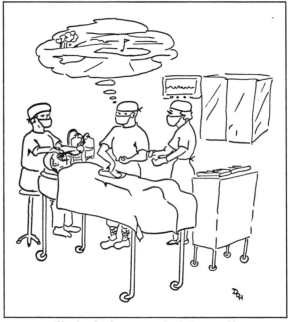

'Number five iron, er – make that a scapel.'

BASIC CONVERSATION

Excuse me: Unnskyld (ewnshewl)
Good morning: God morgen (goo mohrgehn)
Good night: God natt (goo naht)
Good afternoon: God dag (goo dahg)
Good bye: Adjø (ahdyr)
Good day: God dag (goo dahg)
Good evening: God kveld (goo kvehl)
Hello: Hei (hay)

I do not speak Norwegian.
Jeg snakker ikke Norsk
(yay snahkkeh eekeh nohrsk)

I would like ...
Jeg skulle gjerne ha ...
(yay skoolleh yehrneh hah)

I don't understand: Jeg forstår ikke (yay fohrstahr eekeh)
I understand: Jeg forstår (yay fohrstahr)
No: Nei (nay)
Please: Vennligst (vehnligst)

Please bring me ...
Vennligst bring meg ...
(vehnligst breeng may)

Please show me ...
Vennligst vis meg ...
(vehnligst vees may)

Please give me ...
Vennligst gi meg ...
(vehnligst gee may)

See you later: På gjensyn (pah yehnssewn)
See you soon: På gjensyn (pah yehnssewn)
Thank you: Takk (tahk)
Thank you very much: Tusen takk (toosen tahk)
That's alright: Ikke noe å takke for (eekeh noeh ah tahkeh fohr)
Until tomorrow: På morgen (pah mohrgehn)

We would like...
Vi skulle gjerne ha ...
(vee skoolleh yehrneh hah)

Yes: Ja (ya)
Your welcome: Vær så god (vahr sah goo)

(questions)

Can you give me ...?
Kan De gi meg ...?
(kahn dee gee may)

Can I have ...?
Kunne jeg få ...?
(koonneh yay fah)

Can we have ...?
Kunne vi få ...?
(koonneh vee fah)

Can you show me ...?
Kan De vise meg ...?
(kahn dee veesah may)

Can you direct me to ...?
Kan De vise meg veien til ...?
(kahn dee veesah may vaehen teel)

Can you help me please?
Vennligst kan De hjelpe meg?
(vehnligst kahn dee hehlpeh may)

Can you tell me please?
Vennligst kan De fortelle meg?
(vehnligst kahn dee fohrtelleh may)

Do you speak English?
Snakker De engelsk?
(snahkkehr dee eengehlsk)

Do you understand?
Forstår De?
(fohrstahr dee)

Is there anyone here who speaks English?
Er det noen som snakker engelsk her?
(ehr deht noehn sohm snahkkehr eengehlsk heer)

Is there/are there ...?
Er det/er det?
(ehr deht/ehr deht)

AT THE GOLF COURSE

No parking.
Parkering forbudt.
(parkehring fohrboodt)

May I park here?
Kan jeg parkere her?
(kah yay parkereh heer)

Where can I park?
Hvor kan jeg parkere?
(vohr kahn yay parkereh)

Straight ahead.
Rett fram.
(rehtt fram)

To the right.
Til høyre.
(teel hooreh)

To the left.
Til venstre.
(teel vehnstreh)

'Doesn't his gamesmanship make you sick?'

Where is the nearest golf course?
Hvor er nærmeste golfbane?
(vohr ehr naermehsteh golfbahneh)

Is there another golf course near here?
Er det en annen golfbane i nærheten?
(ehr deht een annen golfbahneh ee naerhehtehn)

I would like some information about this course.
Jeg ville gjerne ha noe informasjon om denne banen.
(yay veeleh yehrneh hah noeh informasyon ohm denneh bahnehn)

Do you have any course information in English?
Har dere noe informasjon om denne banen?
(hahr dehreh noeh informasyon ohm denneh bahnehn)

How much is a round of golf?
Hvor mye koster en runde golf?
(vohr meeyeh kohstehr een roondeh golf)

How much are the green fees?
Hvor mye er startavgiften?
(vohr meeyeh ehr startahvgeeftehn)

What is the fee for 9/18 holes?
Hvor mye koster ni/atten hull?
(vohr meeyeh kohstehr nee/otteen hewl)

What is the rate per day/week/month?
Hva er avgiften per dag/uke/måned?
(vah ehr ahvgeeftehn per dahg/ookeh/manehd)

Is there a discount for senior citizens?
Har dere pensjonistrabatt?
(hahr dereh pensyoneestrabaht)

Is there a discount for children?
Har dere rabatt for barn?
(hahr dereh rabaht fohr barn)

Do I need to be a member?
Må jeg være medlem?
(mah yay vaereh mehdlem)

How much is membership?
Hvor mye koster medlemskap?
(vohr meeyeh kohstehr mehdlemskahp)

Per day: Per dag (per dahg)
Per week: Per uke (per ookeh)
Per month: Per måned (per manehd)
Per year: Per år (per ahr)

Do I need to make a reservation?
Er det nødvendig å reservere?
(ehr deht noodvehndeeg ah reservereh)

I have a reservation.
Jeg har reservert.
(yay hahr reservehrt)

My name is ...
Mitt navn er ...
(meet nahvn ehr)

I would like to make a reservation for ...
Jeg vil gjerne reservere for ...
(yay veel yehrneh reservereh fohr)

>   myself: meg selv (may selv)
>   ... people: ... personer (personehr)
>   today: i dag (ee dahg)
>   this afternoon: i ettermiddag (ee ehttermeeddahg)
>   this evening: i kveld (ee kvehl)
>   tomorrow: i morgen (ee mohrgehn)
>   tomorrow morning: i morgen tidlig (ee mohrgehn teedleeg)
>   tomorrow afternoon: i morgen ettermiddag (ee mohrgehn
>   ehttermeeddahg)
>   tomorrow evening: i morgen kveld (ee mohrgehn kvehl)
>   next week: neste uke (nehsteh ookeh)
>
>   on: på (pah)
>   Monday: mandag (mahndahg)
>   Tuesday: tirsdag (teersdahg)
>   Wednesday: onsdag (ohnsdahg)
>   Thursday: torsdag (tohrsdahg)
>   Friday: fredag (freedahg)
>   Saturday: lørdag (lohrdahg)
>   Sunday: søndag (sohndahg)

at: klokka (klokkah)
one o'clock: ett (eht)
one thirty: halv to (halv too)
two o'clock: to (too)
two thirty: halv tre (halv tray)
three o'clock: tre (tray)
three thirty: half fire (halv feereh)
four o'clock: fire (feereh)
four thirty: halv fem (halv fehm)
five o'clock: fem (fehm)
five thirty: halv seks (halv sehks)
six o'clock: seks (sehks)
six thirty: halv sju (halv shew)
seven o'clock: sju (shew)
seven thirty: halv åtte (halv otteh)
eight o'clock: åtte (otteh)
eight thirty: halv ni (halv nee)
nine o'clock: ni (nee)
nine thirty: halv ti (halv tee)
ten o'clock: ti (tee)
ten thirty: halv elleve (halv ehllveh)
eleven o'clock: elleve (ehllveh)
eleven thirty: halv tolv (halv tolv)
twelve o'clock: tolv (tolv)
twelve thirty: halv ett (halv eht)
a.m: morgen/formiddag (mohgehn/fohrmeeddahg)
p.m: ettermiddag/kveld (ehttermeeddahg/kvehl)

Please write it down for me.
Kan De være så snill og skrive det ned for meg?
(kahn dee vaereh sah sneel og skreeveh deht nehd fohr may)

What is the dress code for the course?
Hva slags antrekk må man ha på denne banen?
(vah slags ahntrehk mah man hah pah denneh bahnehn)

Is there night golfing here?
Går det an å spille her om natten?
(gahr deht ahn ah speeleh heer ohm nattehn)

Are U.S. Golf Association rules and regulations used here?
Bruker dere reglene til U.S. Golf Association her?
(brewker dereh regleneh teel yew ehs golf associasheeon heer)

Do you accept tee off times?
Bruker dere starttider?
(brewker dereh startteedehr)

At what time does the course open/close?
Når åpner/stenger banen?
(nahr opnehr/stehngehr bahnehn)

Is there a club house here?
Er det et klubbhus her?
(ehr deht eht klubbhews heer)

At what time does the club house open/close?
Når åpner/stenger klubbhuset?
(nahr opnehr/stehngehr klubbhewseht)

Is there a pro-shop here?
Er det en spesialistbutikk her?
(ehr deht een speseealeestbewteek heer)

At what time does the pro-shop open/close?
Når åpner/stenger spesialistbutikken?
(nah opnehr/stehngehr speseealeestbewteekehn)

Do you need to be a member to use the club house/pro-shop?
Må man være medlem for å kunne bruke klubbhuset/
spesialistbutikken?
(mah man vaereh mehdlem fohr ah kewnneh brewkeh
klubbhewseht/speseealeestbewteekehn)

Is there a putting green/chipping green/driving range?
Har dere putting green/chipping green/driving range?
(hahr dereh putting green/chipping green/driving raenj)

Is there a practice green?
Har dere treningsgreen?
(hahr dereh trayneengsgreen)

Can I get a caddie here?
Kan jeg få tak i en caddie her?
(kahn yay fah tahk ee een kaddee heer)

What is the going rate for a caddie?
Hvor mye koster en caddie?
(vohr meeyeh kohstehr een kaddee)

Do you have a map of the course?
Har De et kart over banen?
(hahr dee eht kahrt over bahnehn)

Where is hole ... located?
Hvor er hull ...?
(vohr ehr hewl)

Can you show me where the ... is located?
Kan du vise meg hvor ...-et lokaliseret?
(kahn dew veeseh may vohr ...-eht lohkahleesehreht)

>   golf club: golfklubb (golfklubb)
>   club house: klubbhus (klubbhews)
>   pro-shop: spesialistbutikk (speseealeestbewteek)

Are spiked shoes required at this course?
Er piggsko påbudt på denne banen?
(ehr peeggskoh pahboodt pah denneh bahnehn)

How long is the course?
Hvor lang er banen?
(vohr lang ehr bahnehn)

9 hole: ni hull (nee hewl)
18 hole: atten hull (otteen hewl)

What is the length of this hole?
Hvor langt er dette hullet?
(vohr lahngt ehr detteh hewlleht)

What is par for this hole?
Hva er par for dette hullet?
(vha ehr pahr fohr detteh hewlleht)

Is there a residential professional at this course?
Er det en fast proff ved denne banen?
(ehr deht een fast proff vehd denneh bahnehn)

What does he/she charge per ½ hour/hour?
Hvor mye tar han/hun per halvtime/time?
(vohr meeyeh tahr hahn/hewn per halvteemeh/teemeh)

PAYING

I would like to pay for ... green fees for ... round(s)/all day.
Jeg skal betale ... startavgifter for ... runder/hele dagen.
(yay skahl beetaleh ... startahvgeeftehr fohr ... rewndehr/heleh dahgen)

Must I pay in advance?
Må jeg betale forskudd?
(mah yay beetaleh fohrskewdd)

May I pay in advance?
Kan jeg betale forskudd?
(kahn yay beetaleh fohrskewdd)

Must I pay cash?
Må jeg betale kontant?
(mah yay beetaleh kontahnt)

May I pay by personal cheque?
Kan jeg betale med sjekk?
(kahn yay beetaleh med chekk)

May I pay with traveller cheques?
Kan jeg betale med reisesjekkar?
(kahn yay beetaleh med raisehchekkahr)

May I pay by credit card?
Kan jeg bruke kredittkort?
(kahn yay brewkeh kredeetkort)

Do you accept ...?
Tar De ...?
(tahr dee ...)

What will the total cost be?
Hvor mye blir det til sammen?
(vohr meeyeh bleer deht teel sammehn)

What is the total cost?
Hvor mye det til sammen?
(vohr meeyeh deht teel sammehn)

We would like to pay separately.
Vi vil gjerne betale hver for oss.
(vee veel yehrneh beetaleh vehr fohr oss)

I only have large bills.
Jeg har bare store sedler.
(yay hahr bareh storeh sehdlehr)

Do you have any change?
Har De vekslepenger?
(hahr dee vehkslehpeengehr)

I would like some small change.
Kan jeg få vekslet til smatt?
(kahn yay fah vehksleht teel smahtt)

Who do I make the cheque out to?
Hvem skal jeg skrive ut sjekken til?
(vehm skahl yay skreeveh ewt chekkehn teel)

Here is my identification.
Her er identifikasjon.
(heer ehr identifikasyon)

bank card: bankkort (bankkort)
driving licence: førerkort (fohrerkort)
passport: pass (pass)

May I have a receipt?
Kan jeg få kvittering på det?
(kahn yay fah kveettehreeng pah deht)

RENTING

I would like to rent ...
Jeg vil gjerne leie ...
(yay veel yehrneh layeh)

We would like to rent ...
Vi vil gjerne leie ...
(vee veel yehrneh layeh)

How much is it to rent (a) ...?
Hvor mye koster det å leie (en) ...?
(vohr meeyeh kohstehr deht ah layeh (een)

Where can I rent a/a pair of ...?
Hvor kan jeg få leid en/et par ...?
(vohr kahn yay fah layd een/eht pahr)

> for ½ hour: i en halvtime (ee een halv teemeh)
> for an hour: i en time (ee een teemeh)
> for a day: i en dag (ee een dahg)

GOLF EQUIPMENT

ball marker(s): ballmerke (ballmerkeh)
box of golf balls: eske golfballer (ehskeh golfballehr)
divot repair tool: green gaffel (green gaffehl)
golf bag: golfbag (golfbag)
golf bag umbrella: golfbag paraply (golfbag parahplew)
golf balls: golfballer (golfballehr)
golf car: golfbil (golfbeel)
golf cart: golfvogn (golfvohgn)
golf clubs: golfkøller (golfkohllehr)
golf club cover: golfkøllecover (golfkohllehkover)
iron: jern (yehrn)
long iron: lang jern (lahng yehrn)
middle iron: middels jern (meeddehls yehrn)
pin: flagg (flag)
pitching wedge: pitching wedge (pitching wehdj)
putter: putter (putter)
rake: rake (rake)
sand wedge: sand wedge (sand wehdj)
score card: poengkort (poehngkort)
shoe spike(s): skopigg (skohpeeg)
shoe spike tool: skrujern (skrewyehrn)
short iron: kort jern (kort yehrn)
tee(s): tee (tee)
wedge: wedge (wehdj)

wood: trekølle (traykohlleh)
wood cover(s): head cover (hehd cover)
wood sock(s): head cover (hehd cover)

CLUBS

1 wood: en tre (een tray)
2 wood: to tre (too tray)
3 wood: tre tre (tray tray)
4 wood: fire tre (feereh tray)
5 wood: fem tre (fehm tray)
6 wood: seks tre (sehks tray)
7 wood: sju tre (shew tray)
8 wood: åtte tre (otteh tray)
9 wood: ni tre (nee tray)
1 iron: en jern (een yehrn)
2 iron: to jern (too yehrn)
3 iron: tre jern (tray yehrn)
4 iron: fire jern (feereh yehrn)
5 iron: fem jern (fehm yehrn)
6 iron: seks jern (sehks yehrn)
7 iron: sju jern (shew yehrn)
8 iron: åtte jern (otteh yehrn)
9 iron: ni jern (nee yehrn)

'Why not cut your losses and count
it as a lost ball.'

GOLF TERMS

slice: høyreskru (hoyrehskrew)
hook: venstreskru (vehnstrehskrew)
Mulligan: Mulligan (mulligan)
handicap: handikap (handeekap)
double bogey: dobbel bogie (dobbehl bogee)
bogey: bogie (bogee)
par: par (par)
birdie: birdie (birdee)
eagle: eagle (eegel)
double eagle: dobbel eagle (dobbehl eegel)

AT THE PRO-SHOP

I am just looking.
Jeg bare ser.
(yay bareh sehr)

I would like to buy ...
Jeg vil gjerne ha ...
(yay veel yehrneh hah)

What size is this?
Hvilken størrelse er dette?
(veelkehn stohrrelseh ehr dehtteh)

What size is that?
Hvilken størrelse er det?
(Veelkehn stohrrelseh ehr deht)

What size are these?
Hvilken størrelse er disse?
(veelkehn stohrrelseh ehr deesseh)

I would like size ...
Jeg vil gjerne ha størrelse ...
(yay veel yehrneh hah stohrrelseh)

I wear size ...
Jeg bruker størrelse ...
(yay brewkehr stohrrelseh)

      extra large: extra stor (extra stohr)
      large: stor (stohr)
      medium: middels (meeddehls)
      small: liten (litehn)
      extra small: extra liten (extra litehn)
      long: lang (lahng)
      short: kort (kort)
      regular: normal (normal)

This is too large.
Det er for stor.
(deht ehr fohr stohr)

This is too small.
Det er for liten.
(deht ehr fohr litehn)

This is too long.
Det er for lang.
(deht ehr fohr lahng)

This is too short.
Det er for kort.
(deht ehr fohr kort)

This is good.
Denne er fin.
(dehnneh ehr feen)

It fits very well.
Den passer helt fint.
(dehn pahssehr hehlt feent)

Do you have a larger size?
Har De større størrelser?
(hahr dee stohrreh stohrrelsehr)

Do you have a smaller size?
Har De en mindre størrelser?
(hahr dee een meendreh stohrrelsehr)

Give me the next size up.
Kan jeg få en størrelse storre?
(kahn yay fah een stohrrelseh stohrreh)

Give me the next size down.
Kan jeg få en størrelse mindre?
(kahn yay fah een stohrrelseh meendreh)

Do you have the same thing in another colour?
Har De denne i andre farger?
(hahr dee dehnneh ee ahndreh fahrgehr)

May I try this on?
Kan jeg prøve denne?
(kahn yay prohveh dehnneh)

Do you have a mirror?
Har De et speil?
(hahr dee eht speel)

Do you have a dressing room?
Har De et prøverom?
(hahr dee eht prohvehroom)

This shoe is too wide.
Denne skoen er for vid.
(dehnneh skohehn ehr fohr veed)

This shoe is too narrow.
Denne skoen er for smal.
(dehnneh skohehn ehr fohr smahl)

These shoes pinch my toes.
Disse skoene trykker på tærne.
(deesseh skohehneh trewkkehr pah taerneh)

I like it.
Jeg liker den.
(yay leekehr dehn)

I don't like it.
Jeg liker den ikke.
(yay leekehr dehn eekeh)

I'll take it.
Jeg tar den.
(yay tahr dehn)

I would like a pair of ...
Jeg ville gjerne ha et par ...
(yay veeleh yehrneh hah eht pahr)

Do you sell ...?
Selger De ...?
(sehlgehr dee)

     golf shoes with/without spikes:
     golfskor med/uten pigge
     (golfskohr med/ewtehn peeggeh)

gloves: hanske (hanskeh)
hats: hatt (hatt)
light jackets: jakker (yakkehr)
trousers: par bukser (pahr bewksehr)
raincoats: regnfrakker (rehgnfrakkehr)

shirts, short/long sleeved:
skjorter, kort/lang erme
(skyortehr, kort/lahng ehrmeh)

shirts with/without a collar/pocket:
skjorter med/uten en krage/lomme
(skyortehr med/ewtehn een krahgeh/lohmmeh)

sunglasses: solbriller (sohlbreellehr)
sweaters: ulljakker/genser
(ewlljakkehr/gehnsehr)
t-shirts: t-skjorter (t-skyortehr)

COLOURS

beige: beige (baysh)
black: svart (svahrt)
blue: blå (blaw)
brown: brun (brewn)
cream: kremfarget (kraymfahrgeht)
crimson: høyrød (hoyrur)
gold: gyllen (yewllern)
green: grønn (grurn)
grey: grå (graw)
orange: oransje (ohrahnsh)
pink: lyserød (lewsser rur)
purple: mørkerød (mewrrker rur)
red: rød (rur)
scarlet: skarlagensrød (skahrlaagernsrur)
silver: sølvfarget (sohlvfahgert)
turquoise: turkis (tewrkees)
white: hvit (veet)
yellow: gul (gewl)

NUMBERS

0: null (nool)
1: en (een)
2: to (too)
3: tre (tray)
4: fire (feereh)
5: fem (fehm)
6: seks (sehks)
7: sju (shew)
8: åtte (otteh)
9: ni (nee)
10: ti (tee)
11: elleve (ehllveh
12: tolv (tolv)
13: tretten (tehttehn)
14: fjorten (fyoortehn)
15: femten (fehmtehn)
16: seksten (saystehn)
17: sytten (sewtehn)
18: atten (ottehn)
19: nitten (neetehn)
20: tjue (kheweh)
21: tjueen (kheweh ayn)
22: tjueto (kheweh too)
23: tjuetre (kheweh tray)
24: tjuefire (kheweh feereh)
25: tjuefem (kheweh fehm)
26: tjueseks (kheweh sehks)
27: tjuesju (kheweh shew)
28: tjueåtte (kheweh otteh)
29: tjueni (kheweh nee)
30: tretti (trehttee)
40: førti (fohrtee)
50: femti (fehmtee)
60: seksti (sehkstee)
70: sytti (sewttee)
80: åtti (ohttee)
90: nitti (neetee)
100: hundre (hewndreh)
150: hundreogfemti (hewndrehog fehmtee)
200: to hundre (too hewndreh)

```
  250: to hundreogfemti (too hewndreh og fehmtee)
  300: tre hundre (tray hewndreh)
  400: fire hundre (feereh hewndreh)
  500: fem hundre (fehm hewndreh)
  600: seks hundre (sehks hewndreh)
  700: sju hundre (shew hewndreh)
  800: åtte hundre (otteh hewndreh)
  900: ni hundre (nee hewndreh)
1,000: tusen (tewsehn)
```

```
 1st: første (fohrshteh)
 2nd: andre (ahndreh)
 3rd: tredje (traydyeh)
 4th: fjerde (fyehrdeh)
 5th: femte (fehmteh)
 6th: sjette (shehteh)
 7th: sjuende (shewehndeh)
 8th: åttende (ottehndeh)
 9th: niende (neeehndeh)
10th: tiende (teeehndeh)
11th: ellevde (ehllehvdeh)
12th: tolvde (tolvdeh)
13th: trettende (trayttehndeh)
14th: fjortende (fyohrtehndeh)
15th: femtende (fehmtehndeh)
16th: sekstende (sehkstehndeh)
17th: syttende (sewtehndeh)
18th: attende (ottehndeh)
```

INTERNATIONAL GOLFERS' LANGUAGE GUIDE

SWEDISH

INTERNATIONELLA GOLFSPELARES SPRÅKGUIDE

SVENSKA

'They say that even the ghost here plays from scratch.'

BASIC CONVERSATION

Excuse me: Ursäkta (ewrsehtah)
Good morning: God morgon (goo morron)
Good night: God natt (goo naht)
Good afternoon: God middag (goo middahg)
Good bye: Adjö (ahyur)
Good day: God dag (goo dahg)
Good evening: God afton (goo ahfton)
Hello: Hej (hey)

I do not speak Swedish.
Jag talar inte Svenska.
(yaag talahr eenteh svehnskah)

I would like ...
Jag skulle vilja ha ...
(yaag skewlleh veelya hah)

I don't understand: Jag förstår inte (yaag fohrstahr eenteh)
I understand: Jag förstår (yaag fohrstahr)
No: Nej (nay)
Please: Var så god (vahr sah goo)

Please bring me ...
Var så god ge mig ...
(vahr sah goo gee may)

Please show me ...
Var så god visa mig ...
(vahr sah goo veesah may)

Please give me ...
Var så god ge mig ...
(vahr sah goo gee may)

See you later: Vi ses (vee says)
See you soon: Vi ses (vee says)
Thank you: Tack (tahk)
Thank you very much: Tack så mycket (tahk sah mewkeht)
That's alright: Det är i orden (deht ahr ee ohrdehn)
Until tomorrow: På morgon (pah morron)

We would like ...
Vi skulle vilja ha ...
(vee skewlleh veelya hah)

Yes: Ja (ya)
Your welcome: Var så god (vahr sah goo)

(questions)

Can you give me ...?
Kan Ni ge mig ...?
(kahn nee gee may)

Can I have ...?
Kunde jag få ...?
(kewndeh yaag fah)

Can we have ...?
Kunde vi få ...?
(kewndeh vee fah)

Can you show me ...?
Kan Ni visa mig ...?
(kahn nee veesah may)

Can you direct me to ...?
Skulle Ni kunna visa mig vägen till ...?
(skewlleh nee kewnnah veesah may vayehn teel)

Can you help me please?
Var så god, skulle Ni kunna hjalpa mig?
(vah sah goo, skewlleh nee kewnnah helpah may)

Can you tell me please?
Var så god, skulle Ni kunna säga mig?
(vahr sah goo, skewlleh nee kewnnah sahgah may)

Do you speak English?
Talar Ni engelska?
(tahlahr nee eengelskah)

Do you understand?
Förstår Ni?
(fohrstahr nee)

Is there anyone here who speaks English?
Finns det någon här som talar engelska?
(feens deht nahgon hahr sohm tahlahr eengelskah)

Is there/are there ...?
Finns det/finns det ...?
(feenns deht/feenns deht)

AT THE GOLF COURSE

No parking.
Parkering förbjuden.
(parkereeng fohrbewden)

May I park here?
Får jag parkera här?
(fahr yaag parkerah hahr)

Where can I park?
Var kan jag parkera?
(vahr kahn yaag parkerah)

Straight ahead.
Rakt fram.
(rahkt fram)

To the right.
Till höger.
(teel hohger)

To the left.
Till vänster.
(teel vahnster)

Where is the nearest golf course?
Var är närmaste golfbana?
(vahr aer nahrmasteh golfbahnah)

Is there another golf course near here?
Finns det en annan golfbana i närheten?
(feenns deht een annahn golfbahnah ee nahrhetehn)

I would like some information about this course.
Jag skulle vilja ha lite information om den här banan.
(yaag skewlleh veelyah ha leeteh informasheeon ohm den hahr
  bahnahn)

Do you have any course information in English?
Kan Ni ge upplysningar på engelska om banan?
(kahn nee gee ewpplewsneengahr pah eengelskah ohm bahnahn)

How much is a round of golf?
Hur mycket kostar en golfrunda?
(hewr mewkeht kohstahr een golfrewndah)

How much are the green fees?
Hur mycket kostar greenavgifterna?
(hewr mewkeht kohstahr greenahvgeefternah)

What is the fee for 9/18 holes?
Vad är avgiften för nio/arton hål?
(vahd aer ahvgeeftehn fohr neeo/ahrton hol)

What is the rate per day/week/month?
Hur mycket kostar det per dag/vecka/månad?
(hewr mewkeht kohstahr deht per dahg/vehka/mahnad)

Is there a discount for senior citizens?
Är det rabatt för pensionärer?
(aer deht rabatt fohr penseeonaerehr)

ıs there a discount for children?
Är det rabatt för barn?
(aer deht rabatt fohr barn)

Do I need to be a member?
Behöver jag vara medlem?
(beehoovehr yaag vahrah mehdlem)

How much is membership?
Hur mycket kostar medlemsskap?
(hewr mewkeht kohstahr mehdlemsskahp)

Per day: per dag (per dahg)
Per week: per vecka (per vehka)
Per month: per månad (per mahnad)
Per year: per år (per ahr)

Do I need to make a reservation?
Behöver jag förhandsbeställa?
(beehoovehr yaag fohrhandsbeestaellah)

I have a reservation.
Jag har bokat.
(yaag hahr bookaht)

My name is ...
Mitt namn är ...
(mitt nahm aer)

I would like to make a reservation for ...
Jag skulle vilja boka för ...
(yaag skewlleh veelyah bookah fohr)

   myself: mig själv (may selv)
   ... people: ... personer (personehr)
   today: idag (eedahg)
   this afternoon: i eftermiddag (ee eftermeeddahg)
   this evening: i kväll (ee kvaell)
   tomorrow: i morgon (ee morron)
   tomorrow morning: i morgon bitti (ee morron beettee)
   tomorrow afternoon: i morgon eftermiddag (ee morron
      eftermeeddahg)
   tomorrow evening: i morgon kväll (ee morron kvaell)
   next week: nästa vecka (naestah vehka)

   on: på (pah)
   Monday: måndag (mondahg)
   Tuesday: tisdag (teesdahg)
   Wednesday: onsdag (ohnsdahg)
   Thursday: torsdag (tohrsdahg)
   Friday: fredag (fraydahg)

Saturday: lördag (loordahg)
Sunday: söndag (soondahg)

at: på (pah)
one o'clock: klockan ett (klohkan eht)
one thirty: klockan halv två (klohkan halv tvoa)
two o'clock: klockan två (klohkan tvoa)
two thirty: klockan halv tre (klohkan halv tray)
three o'clock: klockan tre (klohkan tray)
three thirty: klockan halv fyra (klohkan halv fewrah)
four o'clock: klockan fyra (klohkan fewrah)
four thirty: klockan halv fem (klohkan halv fehm)
five o'clock: klockan fem (klohkan fehm)
five thirty: klockan halv sex (klohkan halv sehks)
six o'clock: klockan sex (klohkan sehks)
six thirty: klockan halv sju (klohkan halv shew)
seven o'clock: klockan sju (klohkan shew)
seven thirty: klockan halv åtta (klohkan halv ottah)
eight o'clock: klockan åtta (klohkan ottah)
eight thirty: klockan halv nio (klohkan halv neeo)
nine o'clock: klockan nio (klohkan neeo)
nine thirty: klockan halv tio (klohkan halv teeo)
ten o'clock: klockan tio (klohkan teeo)
ten thirty: klockan halv elva (klohkan halv ehlvah)
eleven o'clock: klockan elva (klohkan ehlvah)
eleven thirty: klockan halv tolv (klohkan halv tolv)
twelve o'clock: klockan tolv (klohkan tolv)
twelve thirty: klockan halv ett (klohkan halv eht)
a.m: f.m. (ehf em)
p.m: e.m. (eh em)

Please write it down for me.
Var vänlig och skriv ner det för mig.
(vahr vaenleeg ohk skreev nehr deht fohr may)

What is the dress code for the course?
Hur bör man klä sig på den här golfbanan?
(Hewr boor man klah seeg pah den hahr golfbahnahn)

Is there night golfing here?
Spelar man nattgolf här?
(speelahr man nahtgolf haer)

Are U.S. Golf Association rules and regulations used here?
Använder man U.S. Associations regler och bestämmelser här?
(ahnvaendehr man yew ehs assosiasheeons reglehr ohk
  beestaemmelsehr haer)

Do you accept tee off times?
Accepteras starttider här?
(aksepterahs startteedehr haer)

At what time does the course open/close?
Hur dags öppnas/stängs golfbanan?
(hewr dahgs ohppnas/staengs golfbahnahn)

Is there a club house here?
Finns det ett klubbhus här?
(feenns deht eht klewbbhews haer)

At what time does the club house open/close?
Hur dags öppnas/stängs klubbhuset?
(hewr dahgs ohppnas/staengs klewbbhewset)

Is there a pro-shop here?
Finns det en golfshop här?
(feenns deht een golfshop haer)

At what time does the pro-shop open/close?
Hur dags öppnas/stängs golfshoppen?
(hewr dahgs ohppnas/staengs golfshoppen)

Do you need to be a member to use the club house/pro-shop?
Behöver man vara medlem för att använda klubbhuset/
  golfshoppen?
(beehoover man vahrah mehdlem fohr aht ahnvaenda
  klewbbhewset/golfshoppen)

Is there a putting green/chipping green/driving range?
Finns det en inslagsplats/chipping green/utslagsplats?
(feenns deht een eenslkahgsplahts/chipping green/
  ewtslahgsplahts)

Is there a practice green?
Finns det en övningsbana?
(feenns deht een ohvneengsbahnah)

Can I get a caddie here?
Kan jag få en caddie här?
(kah yaag fah een kaddee haer)

What is the going rate for a caddie?
Vad är det gängse priset för en caddie?
(vahd aer deht gaengseh preeseht fohr een kaddee)

Do you have a map of the course?
Har Ni en karta över golfbanan?
(hahr nee een kartah ohver golfbahnahn)

Where is hole ... located?
Var är hål ... placerat?
(vahr aer hol ... plaseraht)

Can you show me where the ... is located?
Kan Ni visa mig var ... ligger?
(kahn nee veesah may vahr ... leeggehr)

golf club: golfklubb (golfklewbb)
club house: klubbhus (klewbbhews)
pro-shop: golfshop (golfshop)

Are spiked shoes required at this course?
Behöver man golfskor på den här banan?
(beehoover man golfskohr pah den haer bahnahn)

How long is the course?
Hur lång är banan?
(hewr lahng aer bahnahn)

9 hole: nio hål (neeo hol)
18 hole: arton hål (ahrton hol)

What is the length of this hole?
Hur långt är det här hålet?
(hewr lahngt aer deht haer holeht)

What is par for this hole?
Vad är par för det här hålet?
(vahd aer par fohr deht haer holeht)

Is there a residential professional at this course?
Finns det en anställd professionell tränare här på den här banan?
(feenns deht een ahnstaelld professeeonell traenareh haer pah den
haer bahnahn)

What does he/she charge per ½ hour/hour?
Vad tar han/hon betalt per halvtimme/timme?
(vahd tahr hahn/hohn beetahlt per halvteemmeh/teemmeh)

PAYING

I would like to pay for ... green fees for ... round(s)/all day.
Jag skulle vilja betala för ... greenavgifter for ... golfrundor/hela
dagen.
(yaag skewlleh veelya beetalah fohr ... greenahvgeefter for ...
golfrewndor helah dahgen)

Must I pay in advance?
Måste jag betala i förskott?
(mahsteh yaag beetalah ee fohrskohtt)

May I pay in advance?
Får jag betala i förskott?
(fahr yaag beetalah ee fohrskohtt)

Must I pay cash?
Måste jag betala kontant?
(mahsteh yaag beetalah kontant)

May I pay by personal cheque?
Kan jag betala med check?
(kahn yaag beetalah med check)

May I pay with traveller cheques?
Kan jag betala med rese checkar?
(kahn yaag beetalah med rehseh checkahr)

May I pay by credit card?
Kan jag betala med kreditkort?
(kahn yaag beetalah med kreditkort)

Do you accept ...?
Tar Ni ...?
(tahr nee ...)

What will the total cost be?
Hur mycket kommer det att kosta allt som allt?
(hewr mewkeht kommehr deht aht kostah ahlt som ahlt)

What is the total cost?
Hur mycket kostar det allt som allt?
(hewr mewkeht kostahr deht ahlt som ahlt)

We would like to pay separately.
Vi skulle vilja betala var och en för sig.
(vee skewlleh veelya beetalah vahr ohk een fohr seeg)

I only have large bills.
Jag har bara stora sedlar.
(yaag hahr barah storah sehdlar)

Do you have any change?
Har Ni växel?
(hahr nee vaeksel)

I would like some small change.
Jag skulle vilja ha lite växelpengar.
(yaag skewlleh veelya hah liteh vaekselpengar)

Who do I make the cheque out to?
Till vem ska jag skriva ut checken?
(teel vehm skah yaag skreevah ewt checken)

Here is my identification.
Här är min legitimation.
(haer aer meen legitimasheeon)

bank card: kreditkort (kreditkort)
driving licence: körkort (kohrkort)
passport: pass (pass)

May I have a receipt?
Kan jag få kvitto?
(kahn yaag fah kveettoh)

RENTING

I would like to rent ...
Jag skulle vilja hyra ...
(yaag skewlleh veelya hewrah)

We would like to rent ...
Vi skulle vilja hyra ...
(vee skewlleh veelya hewrah)

How much is it to rent (a) ...?
Hur mycket kostar det at hyra ...
(hewr mewkeht kostahr deht aht hewrah)

Where can I rent a/a pair of ...?
Var kan jag hyra ett/ett par ...
(vahr kahn yaag hewrah eht/eht pahr)

> for ½ hour: för en halvtimme (fohr een halvteemmeh)
> for an hour: för en timme (fohr een timmeh)
> for a day: för en dag (fohr een dahg)

GOLF EQUIPMENT

ball marker(s): bollmarkering(ar) (bohllmarkering(ahr)
box of golf balls: låda golfbollar (lahdah golfbohllahr)
divot repair tool: greenlagare (greenlagareh)
golf bag: golfväska (golfvaeskah)
golf bag umbrella: paraply för golfväska (pahraplew fohr golfvaeskah)
golf balls: golfbollar (golfbohllahr)
golf car: golfvagn (golfvahgn)
golf cart: golfkärra (golfkaerrah)
golf clubs: golfklubbor (golfklewbbohr)
golf club cover: klubbhuvudskydd (klewbbhoovoodskewdd)
iron: järnklubba (yaernklewbba)
long iron: lång järnklubba (lahng yaernklewbba)
middle iron: medeljärnklubba (medelyaernklewbba)
pin: flagga (flaggah)
pitching wedge: p-wedge (pee-vehdj)
putter: putter (putter)
rake: kratta (krattah)

sand wedge: s-wedge (ehs-vehdj)
score card: scorekort (skorekort)
shoe spike(s): skobrodd (ar) skohbrodd (ahr)
shoe spike tool: skobroddsverktyg (skohbroddsvehrktewg)
short iron: kort järnklubba (kort yaernklewbba)
tee(s): tee (tee)
wedge: wedge (vehdj)
wood: träklubba (traeklewbba)
wood cover(s): träklubbsskydd (traeklewbbskewdd)
wood sock(s): träklubbssocka(or) (traeklewbbssockah(ohr)

CLUBS

1 wood: träklubba ett (traeklewbba eht)
2 wood: träklubba två (traeklewbba tvoa)
3 wood: träklubba tre (traeklewbba tray)
4 wood: träklubba fyra (traeklewbba fewrah)
5 wood: träklubba fem (traeklewbba fehm)
6 wood: träklubba sex (traeklewbba sehks)
7 wood: träklubba sju (traeklewbba shew)
8 wood: träklubba åtte (traeklewbba ottah)
9 wood: träklubba nio (traeklewbba neeo)
1 iron: järnklubba ett (yaernklewbba eht)
2 iron: järnklubba två (yaernklewbba tvoa)
3 iron: järnklubba tre (yaernklewbba tray)
4 iron: järnklubba fyra (yaernklewbba fewrah)
5 iron: järnklubba fem (yaernklewbba fehm)
6 iron: järnklubba sex (yaernklewbba sehks)
7 iron: järnklubba sju (yaernklewbba shew)
8 iron: järnklubba åtte (yaernklewbba ottah)
9 iron: järnklubba nio (yaernklewbba neeo)

GOLF TERMS

slice: slice (slais)
hook: hook (hook)
Mulligan: Mulligan (mulligan)
handicap: handicap (handikap)
double bogey: dubbelbogie (dewbbelboggee)
bogey: bogie (bogee)
par: par (par)

birdie: birdie (birdee)
eagle: eagle (eegel)
double eagle: albatross (albatross)

AT THE PRO-SHOP

I am just looking.
Jag bara tittar.
(yaag barah teettahr)

I would like to buy ...
Jag skulle vilja köpa ...
(yaag skewlleh veelyah koopah)

What size is this?
Vilken storlek är det här?
(veelkehn stohrlehk aer deht haer)

What size is that?
Vilken storlek är det där?
(veelkehn stohlehk aer deht daer)

What size are these?
Vilken storlek är de här?
(veelkehn stohrlehk aer dee haer)

I would like size ...
Jag skulle vilja ha storlek ...
(yaag skewlleh veelyah hah stohrlehk)

I wear size ...
Jag har storlek ...
(yaag hahr stohrlehk)

    extra large: extra stor (extra stohr)
    large: stor (stohr)
    medium: medelmåttig (medelmahtteeg)
    small: liten (leetehn)
    extra small: extra liten (extra leetehn)
    long: lång (lahng)
    short: kort (kort)
    regular: normal (normal)

This is too large.
Denna är för stor.
(dehnnah aer fohr stohr)

This is too small.
Denna är för liten.
(dehnnah aer fohr leetehn)

This is too long.
Denna är för lång.
(dehnnah aer fohr lahng)

This is too short.
Denna är för kort.
(dehnnah aer fohr kort)

This is good.
Det är bra.
(deht aer brah)

'You must admit he's got style!'

It fits very well.
Den/det passar mycket bra.
(dehn/deht passahr mewkeht brah)

Do you have a larger size?
Har Ni en större storlek?
(hahr nee een stohrreh stohrlehk)

Do you have a smaller size?
Har Ni en mindre storlek?
(hahr nee een meendreh stohrlehk)

Give me the next size up.
Ge mig en storlek större.
(gee may een stohrlehk stohrreh)

Give me the next size down.
Ge mig en storlek mindre.
(gee may een stohrlehk meendreh)

Do you have the same thing in another colour?
Har Ni samma sak i en annan färg?
(hahr nee sammah sahk ee een ahnnan fahrg)

May I try this on?
Kan jag prova den här?
(kahn yaag prohvah dehn haer)

Do you have a mirror?
Har Ni en spegel?
(hahr nee een speegehl)

Do you have a dressing room?
Har Ni ett provrum?
(hahr nee ehtt provroom)

This shoe is too wide.
Den här skon är för bred.
(dehn haer skohn aer fohr brehd)

This shoe is too narrow.
Den här skon är för trång.
(dehn haer skohn aer fohr trahng)

These shoes pinch my toes.
Dom här skorna klämmer i tårna.
(dohm haer skohrnah klaemmehr ee tahrnah)

I like it.
Jag tycker om det.
(yaag tewkher ohm deht)

I don't like it.
Jag tycker inte om det.
(yaag tewkher eenteh ohm deht)

I'll take it.
Jag tar det.
(yaag tahr deht)

I would like a pair of ...
Jag skulle vilja ha ett par ...
(yaag skewlleh veelyah hah ehtt pahr)

Do you sell ...?
Säljar Ni ...?
(saelyahr nee)

golf shoes with/without spikes:
golfskor med/utan skobroddar
(golfskohr med/ewtahn skohbroddahr)

gloves: handskar (handskahr)
hats: hatt (hatt)
light jackets: jakker (yakkehr)
pants (trousers): långbyxor (lahngbewksohr)
raincoats: regnrockar (rehgeenrokkahr)

shirts, short/long sleeved:
skjortar, kort/lång ärm
(skyohrtahr, kort/lahng aerm)

shirts with/without a collar/pocket:
skjortar med/utan en krage/ficka
(skyohrtahr med/ewtahn een krahgeh/feekah)

sunglasses: solglasögon (sohlglahsohgohn)
sweaters: tröjar (trohyahr)
t-shirts: t-skjortar (t-skyohrtahr)

COLOURS

beige: beige (baysh)
black: svart (svahrt)
blue: blå (bloa)
brown: brun (brewn)
cream: krämfärgad (kraemfaergahd)
crimson: knallröd (knahlrurd)
gold: guldfärgad (gewldfaergahd)
green: grön (gruhn)
grey: grå (groa)
orange: brandgul (brahndgewl)
pink: rosa (rosah)
purple: violett (veeooleht)
red: röd (rurd)
scarlet: scharlakansröd (shahlaakahnsrurd)
silver: silverfärgad (silverfaergahd)
turquoise: turkosblå (tewrkoosbloa)
white: vit (veet)
yellow: gul (gewl)

NUMBERS

0: noll (nohll)
1: ett (eht)
2: två (tvoa)
3: tre (tray)
4: fyra (fewrah)
5: fem (fehm)
6: sex (sehks)
7: sju (shew)
8: åtta (ottah)
9: nio (neeo)
10: tio (teeo)
11: elva (ehvah)
12: tolv (tolv)
13: tretton (trehton)
14: fjorton (fyoorton)
15: femton (fehmton)
16: sexton (sehkston)
17: sjutton (shewton)
18: arton (ahrton)
19: nitton (neeton)
20: tjugo (khewgoo)

'All right, who coughed?'

21: tjugoett (khewgooeht)
22: tjugotvå (thewgootvoa)
23: tjugotre (khewgootray)
24: tjugofyra (khewgoofewrah)
25: tjugofem (khewgoofehm)
26: tjugosex (khewgoosehks)
27: tjugosju (khewgooshew)
28: tjugoåtta (khewgooottah)
29: tjugonio (khewgooneeo)
30: trettio (threhteeo)
40: fyrtio (fewrteeo)
50: femtio (fehmteeo)
60: sextio (sehksteeo)
70: sjuttio (shewteeo)
80: åttio (otteeo)
90: nittio (neetteeo)
100: hundra (hewndrah)
150: hundrafemtio (hewndrahfehmteeo)
200: tvåhundra (tvoahewndrah)
250: tvåhundrafemtio (tvoahewndrahfehmteeo)
300: trehundra (trayhewndrah

```
  400: fyrahundra (fewrahhewdrah)
  500: femhundra (fehmhewndrah)
  600: sexhundra (sehkshewndrah)
  700: sjuhundra (shewhewndrah)
  800: åttahundra (ottahhewndrah)
  900: niohundra (neeohewndrah)
1,000: tusen (tewsehn)
```

```
 1st: första (foorstah)
 2nd: andra (ahndrah)
 3rd: tredje (traydyer)
 4th: fjärde (fyaerder)
 5th: femte (fehmter)
 6th: sjätte (shehter)
 7th: sjunde (shewnder)
 8th: åttonde (ottonder)
 9th: nionde (neeonder)
10th: tionde (teeonder)
11th: elvde (ehlvder)
12th: tolvde (tolvder)
13th: trettonde (trehttonder)
14th: fjortonde (fyohrtonder)
15th: femtonde (fehmtohnder)
16th: sextonde (sehkstohnder)
17th: sjuttonde (shewttonder)
18th: artonde (ahrtonder)
```

INTERNATIONAL GOLFERS' LANGUAGE GUIDE

DANISH

INTERNATIONAL GOLFSPILLERS SPROGFØRER

DANSK

'Whose bright idea was it to bring our wives?'

BASIC CONVERSATION

Excuse me: Undskyld (ewnskewl)
Good morning: Godmorgen (goad mohrehn)
Good night: Godnat (goadnaht)
Good afternoon: Goddag (goaddai)
Good bye: Farvel (fahrvehl)
Good day: Goddag (goaddai)
Good evening: Godaften (goadahftehn)
Hello: Hej (hay)

I do not speak Danish.
Jeg taler ikke dansk.
(yeeg tahlehr eekkeh dahnsk)

I would like ...
Jeg vil gerne ha ...
(yeeg veel yehrneh hah)

I don't understand: Jeg forstår ikke (yeeg fohrstahr eekkeh)
I understand: Jeg forstår (yeeg fohrstahr)
No: Nej (nay)
Please: Vær så venlig (vehr sah vehnlee)

Please bring me ...
Vær så venlig bring mig ...
(vehr sah vehnlee breeng meeg)

Please show me ...
Vær så venlig vis mig ...
(Vehr sah vehnlee vees meeg)

Please give me ...
Vær så venlig giv mig ...
(Vehr sah vehnlee geev meeg)

See you later: På gensyn (pah gehnsewn)
See you soon: På gensyn (pah gehnsewn)
Thank you: Tak (tahk)
Thank you very much: Mange Tak (mangeh tahk)
That's alright: Det er i orden (day ehr ee ohrdehn)
Until tomorrow: På morgen (pah mohrehn)

We would like ...
Vi vil gerne ha ...
(vee veel yehrneh hah)

Yes: Ja (yah)
Your welcome: Åh, jeg be'r (ah, yeeg beher)

(questions)

Can you give me ...?
Kan De giv mig ...?
(kahn dee geev meeg)

Can I have ...?
Kan jeg få ...?
(kahn yeeg fah)

Can we have ...?
Kan vi få ...?
(kahn vee fah)

Can you show me ...?
Kan De vise mig ...?
(kahn dee veeseh meeg)

Can you direct me to ...?
Kan De vise mig vejen til ...?
(kahn dee veeseh meg vayeen teel)

Can you help me please?
Vær så venlig, kan De hjælpe mig?
(vehr sah vehnlee, kahn dee helpeh meeg)

Can you tell me please?
Vær så venlig, kan De sige mig?
(vehr sah vehnlee, kahn dee seegeh meeg)

Do you speak English?
Taler De engelsk?
(tahlehr dee eengehlsk)

Do you understand?
Forstår De?
(fohrstahr dee)

Is there anyone here who speaks English?
Er der nogen her, der taler engelsk?
(ehr dehr nohgehn heer, dehr tahlehr eengehlsk)

Is there/are there ...?
Er der/Er der ...?
(ehr dehr/ehr dehr)

AT THE GOLF COURSE

No parking.
Ingen parkering
(eengehn parkereeng)

May I park here?
Må jeg parkere her?
(mah yeeg parkereh heer)

Where can I park?
Hvor kan jeg parkere?
(vhor kahn yeeg parkereh)

Straight ahead.
Lige fremad.
(leegeh freemahd)

To the right.
Til højre
(teel hohyreh)

To the left.
Til venstre
(teel vehnstreh)

Where is the nearest golf course?
Hvor er den nærmeste golfbane?
(vhor ehr dehn nehrmehsteh golfbahneh)

Is there another golf course near here?
Er der en anden golfbane i nærheden?
(ehr dehr een ahndehn golfbahneh ee nehrhehdehn)

I would like some information about this course.
Jeg ville gerne have nogle oplysninger om denne golfbane.
(yeeg veelleh yehrneh haveh nohgleh ohplewsneengehr ohm
    dehnneh golfbahneh)

Do you have any course information in English?
Har De nogen oplysninger om banen på engelsk?
(hahr dee nohgehn ohplewsneengehr ohm bahnehn pah
    eengehlsk)

How much is a round of golf?
Hvad koster en runde golf?
(vahd kohstehr een rewndeh golf)

How much are the green fees?
Hvor meget er Deres green fee?
(vhor mehgeht ehr deerees green fee)

What is the fee for 9/18 holes?
Hvad koster ni huller/atten huller?
(vahd kohstehr nee hewllehr/ahtteen hewllehr)

What is the rate per day/week/month?
Hvad er raten per dag/uge/måned?
(vahd ehr rahtehn per dai/ewgeh/mahnehd)

Is there a discount for senior citizens?
Gives der rabat til pensionister?
(geevehs dehr rahbaht teel penseeoneestehr)

Is there a discount for children?
Gives der rabat til børn?
(geevehs dehr rahbaht teel bohrn)

Do I need to be a member?
Behøver jeg at være medlem?
(beehohvveer yeeg aht vehreh mehdlem)

How much is membership?
Hvad koster det at blive medlem?
(vahd kohstehr day aht bleeveh mehdlem)

Per day: Per dag (per dai)
Per week: Per uge (per ewgeh)
Per month: Per måned (per mahned)
Per year: per år (per ahr)

Do I need to make a reservation?
Behøver jeg at reservere plads?
(beehohveer yeeg aht reservereh plahds)

I have a reservation.
Jeg har en reservation.
(yeeg hahr een reservation)

My name is ...
Mit navn er ...
(meet nahvn ehr)

I would like to make a reservation for ...
Jeg vil gerne reservere tid til ...
(yeeg veel yehrneh reservereh teed teel)

> myself: mig selv (meeg sehlv)
> ... people: ... mennesker (mehnnehskehr)
> today: i dag (ee dai)
> this afternoon: i eftermiddag (ee ehftehrmeeddai)
> this evening: i aften (ee ahftehn)
> tomorrow: i morgen (ee mohrehn)
> tomorrow morning: i morgen tidlig (ee mohrehn teedleeg)
> tomorrow afternoon: i morgen eftermiddag (ee mohrehn ehftehrmeeddai)
> tomorrow evening: i morgen aften (ee mohrehn ahftehn)
> next week: næste uge (nehsteh engeh)
>
> on: på (pah)
> Monday: Mandag (mahndai)
> Tuesday: Tirsdag (teersdai)
> Wednesday: Onsdag (oansdai)
> Thursday: Torsdag (toarsdai)
> Friday: Fredag (fraydai)

Saturday: Lørdag (lohrdai)
Sunday: Søndag (sohndai)

at: på (pah)
one o'clock: klokken et (klohkkehn eht)
one thirty: et tredive (eht traiver)
two o'clock: klokken to (klohkkehn too)
two thirty: to tredive (too traiver)
three o'clock: klokken tre (klohkkehn tray)
three thirty: tre tredive (tray traiver)
four o'clock: klokken fire (klohkkehn feereh)
four thirty: fire tredive (feereh traiver)
five o'clock: klokken fem (klohkkehn fehn)
five thirty: fem tredive (fehm traiver)
six o'clock: klokken seks (klohkkehn sayks)
six thirty: seks tredive (sayks traiver)
seven o'clock: klokken syv (klohkkehn sewv)
seven thirty: syv tredive (sewv traiver)
eight o'clock: klokken otte (klohkkehn ohtteh)
eight thirty: otte tredive (ohtteh traiver)
nine o'clock: klokken ni (klohkkehn nee)
nine thirty: ni tredive (nee traiver)
ten o'clock: klokken ti (klohkkehn tee)
ten thirty: ti tredive (tee traiver)
eleven o'clock: klokken elleve (klohkkehn aylveh)
eleven thirty: elleve tredive (aylveh traiver)
twelve o'clock: klokken tolv (klohkkehn toal)
twelve thirty: tolv tredive (toal traiver)
a.m: før tolv frokost (fohr toal frohkost)
p.m: efter tolv frokost (ehftehr toal frohkost)

Please write it down for me.
Vær venlig at skrive det ned for mig.
(vehr vehnlee aht skreeveh day nehd fohr meeg)

What is the dress code for the course?
Er der påklædningsregler for denne bane?
(ehr dehr pahklehdneengsrehglehr fohr dehnneh bahneh)

Is there night golfing here?
Kan man spille her om aftenen?
(kahn man speeleh heer ohm ahfteenehn)

Are U.S. Golf Association rules and regulations used here?
Benyttes U.S. Golf Association regler og regulationer her?
(beenewttehs yew ehs golf assosiation rehglehr oh regulationehr
  heer)

Do you accept tee off times?
Kan De acceptere tee off tider?
(kahn dee aksehptereh tee off teedehr)

At what time does the course open/close?
Hvornår åbner/lukker banen?
(vohrnahr obnehr/lewkkehr bahnehn)

Is there a club house here?
Er der et klubhus her?
(ehr dehr eht klewbhews heer)

At what time does the club house open/close?
Hvad tid åbner/lukker klubhuset?
(vahd teed obnehr/lewkkehr klewbhewseht)

Is there a pro-shop here?
Har De en udstyrsforretning her?
(hahr dee een ewdstewrsfohrrehtneeng heer)

At what time does the pro-shop open/close?
Hvad tid åbner/lukker udstyrsforretningen?
(vahd teed obnehr/lewkkehr ewdstewrsfohrrehtneengehn)

Do you need to be a member to use the club house/pro-shop?
Behøver man at være medlem for at benytte klubhuset/
  udstyrsforretningen?
(beehohveer man aht vehreh mehdlem fohr aht beenewtteh
  klewbhewseht/ewdstewrsfohrrehtnengehn)

Is there a putting green/chipping green/driving range?
Har De en putting green/chipping green/drivingbane?
(hahr dee een putting green/chipping green/driving bahnneh)

Is there a practice green?
Har De en træningsgreen?
(hahr dee een trehneengsgreen)

Can I get a caddie here?
Kan jeg få en caddy her?
(kahn yeeg fah een kaddee heer)

What is the going rate for a caddie?
Hvad er det normale gebyr for en caddy?
(vahd ehr day normaleh geebewr fohr een kaddee)

Do you have a map of the course?
Har De et kort over banen?
(hahr dee eht kort over bahnehn)

Where is hole ... located?
Hvor er hul ... placeret?
(vohr ehr hewl ... plahsehret)

Can you show me where the ... is located?
Kan De vise mig hvor ... er placeret?
(kahn dee veeseh meeg vohr ... ehr plahsehreht)

     golf club: golfklub (golfklewb)
     club house: klubhus (klewbhews)
     pro-shop: udstyrsforretning (ewdstewrsfohrrehtneengehn)

Are spiked shoes required at this course?
Behøver man at bruge pigsko på denne bane?
(beehohveer man aht brewgeh peegskoh pah dehnneh bahneh)

How long is the course?
Hvor lang er banen?
(vohr lahng ehr bahnehn)

     9 hole: ni huller (nee hewllehr)
     18 hole: atten huller (ahtdern hewllehr)

What is the length of this hole?
Hvad er længden på dette hul?
(vahd ehr lehngdehn pah dehtteh hewl)

What is par for this hole?
Hvad er par for dette hul?
(vahd ehr par fohr dehtteh hewl)

Is there a residential professional at this course?
Har De en fast træner på denne bane?
(hahr dee een fast trehnehr pah dehnneh bahneh)

What does he/she charge per ½ hour/hour?
Hvad tager han/hende i gebyr per halvtime/time?
(vahd tahgehr hahn/hehndeh ee geebewr per hahlvteemeh/
    teemeh)

PAYING

I would like to pay for ... green fees for ... round(s)/all day.
Jeg vil gerne betale for ... green gebyr for ... runder/hele dagen.
(yeeg veel yehrneh beetahleh fohr ... green geebewr fohr ...
    rewndehr/hehleh daiehn)

Must I pay in advance?
Skal jeg betale forud?
(skahl yeeg beetahleh fohrewd)

May I pay in advance?
Må jeg betale forud?
(mah yeeg beetahleh fohrewd)

Must I pay cash?
Skal jeg betale kontant?
(skahl yeeg beetahleh kohntant)

May I pay by personal cheque?
Må jeg betale med min personlige check?
(mah yeeg beetahleh med meen personleegeh check)

May I pay with traveller cheques?
Må jeg betale med traveller check?
(mah yeeg beetahleh med traveller check)

May I pay by credit card?
Må jeg betale med kreditkort?
(mah yeeg beetahleh med kreditkort)

Do you accept ...?
Akcepterer De ...?
(aksehpterehr dee ...)

What will the total cost be?
Hvad vil det beløbe sig till i alt?
(vahd veel day beelohbeh seeg teel ee ahlt)

What is the total cost?
Hvad er det beløbe i alt?
(vahd ehr day beelohbeh ee ahlt)

We would like to pay separately.
Vi vil gerne betale hver for sig.
(vee veel yehrneh beetahleh vehr fohr seeg)

I only have large bills.
Jeg har kun store sedler.
(yeeg hahr kewn stohreh sehdlehr)

Do you have any change?
Kan De veksle?
(kahn dee vehksleh)

I would like some small change.
Jeg vil gerne have nogen småpenge.
(yeeg veel yehrneh hahveh nohgehn smahpehngeh)

Who do I make the cheque out to?
Hvem skal jeg udstede checken til?
(vehm skahl yeeg ewdstehdeh checkehn teel)

Here is my identification.
Her er min identificering.
(heer ehr meen identifisehreeng)

bank card: bankkort (bahnkkort)
driving licence: kørekort (kohrehkort)
passport: pas (pahs)

May I have a receipt?
Må jeg bede om en kvittering?
(mah yeeg beedeh ohm een kveettehreeng)

RENTING

I would like to rent ...
Jeg ville gerne leje ...
(yeeg veeleh yehrneh layeh)

We would like to rent ...
Vi ville gerne leje ...
(vee veelleh yehrneh layeh)

How much is it to rent (a) ...?
Hvad koster det at leje (en) ...
(vahd kohstehr day aht layeh (een)

Where can I rent a/a pair of ...?
Hvor kan jeg leje en/et par ...
(vohr kahn yeeg layeh een/eht pahr)

> for ½ hour: i en halv time (ee een hahlv teemeh)
> for an hour: i en time (ee een teemeh)
> for a day: i en dag (ee een dai)

GOLF EQUIPMENT

ball marker(s): boldafmærkere (bohldahfmehrkehreh)
box of golf balls: æske golfbolde (ehskeh golfbohldeh)
divot repair tool: græstørv reparationsredskab (grehstohrv reparationsrehdskahb)
golf bag: golftaske (golftahskeh)
golf bag umbrella: golftaskeparaply (golftahskehpahraplew)
golf balls: golfbolde (golfbohldeh)
golf car: golfbil (golfbeel)
golf cart: golfvogn (golfvohgeen)
golf clubs: golfkøller (golfkohllehr)
golf club cover: golfkølleovertræk (golfkohllehrovertrehk)
iron: jernkølle (yehrnkohlleh)
long iron: lang jernkølle (lahng yehrnkohlleh)
middle iron: mellem jernkølle (mehllehm yehrnkohlleh)
pin: flagstang (flagstahng)
pitching wedge: pitch wedge (pitch wehdj)
putter: putter (putter)
rake: rive (reeveh)

sand wedge: sand wedge (sand wehdj)
score card: poengkort (poehngkort)
shoe spike(s): skopigge (skohpeeggeh)
shoe spike tool: nøgle til skopigge (nohgleh teel skohpeeggeh)
short iron: kort jernkølle (kort yehrnkohlleh)
tee(s): tee(r) (tee(r)
wedge: wedge (wehdj)
wood: trækølle (trehkohlleh)
wood cover(s): trækølleovertræk(ker) (trehkohllehovertrehk(kehr)
wood sock(s): trækøllesok(ker) (trehkohllehsohk(kehr)

CLUBS

1 wood: en trækølle (ehn trehkohlleh)
2 wood: to trækølle too trehkohlleh)
3 wood: tre trækølle (tray trehkohlleh)
4 wood: fire trækølle (feereh trehkolleh)
5 wood: fem trækølle (fehm trehkolleh)
6 wood: seks trækølle (sayks trehkolleh)
7 wood: syv trækølle (sewv trehkolleh)
8 wood: otte trækølle (ohtteh trehkolleh)
9 wood: ni trækølle (nee trehkolleh)

1 iron: en jernkølle (ehn yehrnkohlleh)
2 iron: to jernkølle (too yehrnkohlleh)
3 iron: (tre jernkølle (tray yehrnkohlleh)
4 iron: fire jernkølle (feereh yehrnkohlleh)
5 iron: fem jernkølle (fehm yehrnkohlleh)
6 iron: seks jernkølle (sayks yehrnkohlleh)
7 iron: syv jernkølle (sewv yehrnkohlleh)
8 iron: otte jernkølle (ohtteh yehrnkohlleh)
9 iron: ni jernkølle (nee yehrnkohlleh)

GOLF TERMS

slice: slice (slice)
hook: hook (hook)
Mulligan: Mulligan (mulligan)
handicap: handicap (hadikap)
double bogey: double bogie (doubleh bogee)
bogey: bogie (bogee)
par: par (par)

birdie: birdie (birdee)
eagle: eagle (eegel)
double eagle: double eagle (doubleh eegel)

AT THE PRO-SHOP

I am just looking.
Jeg kigger bare.
(yeeg keeggehr bahreh)

I would like to buy ...
Jeg ville gerne købe ...
(yeeg veelleh yehrneh kohbeh)

What size is this?
Hvad størrelse er denne?
(vahd stohrrehlseh ehr dehnneh)

What size is that?
Hvad størrelse er den?
(vahd stohrrehlseh ehr dehn)

What size are these?
Hvad størrelse er disse?
(vahd stohrrehlseh ehr deesseh)

I would like size ...
Jeg ville gerne størrelse ...
(yeeg veelleh yehrneh stohrrehlseh)

I wear size ...
Jeg bruger størrelse ...
(yeeg brewgehr stohrrehlseh)

    extra large: extra store (extra stohreh)
    large: store (stohreh)
    medium: middel (meeddehl)
    small: små (smah)
    extra small: extra små (extra smah)
    long: lang (lahng)
    short: kort (kort)
    regular: normal (normal)

This is too large.
Den er for store.
(dehn ehr fohr stohreh)

This is too small.
Den er for små.
(dehn ehr fohr smah)

This is too long.
Den er for lang.
(dehn ehr fohr lahng)

This is too short.
Den er for kort.
(dehn ehr fohr kort.)

This is good.
Den er god.
(dehn ehr goad)

It fits very well.
Den passer fint.
(dehn pahssehr feent)

'If I get this right we can get there before the flag catches fire.'

Do you have a larger size?
Har De en større størrelse?
(hahr dee een stohrreh stohrrehlseh)

Do you have a smaller size?
Har De en mindre størrelse?
(hahr dee een meendreh stohrrehlseh)

Give me the next size up.
Giv mig en størrelse større.
(geev meeg een stohrrehlseh stohrreh)

Give me the next size down.
Giv mig en størrelse mindre.
(geev meeg een stohrrehlseh meendreh)

Do you have the same thing in another colour?
Har De den i en anden farve?
(hahr dee dehn ee een ahndehn fahrveh)

May I try this on?
Må jeg prøve om den passer?
(mah yeeg prohveh ohm dehn pahssehr)

Do you have a mirror?
Har De et spejl?
(hahr dee eht speeyl)

Do you have a dressing room?
Har De et prøveværelse?
(hahr dee eht prohvehvehrehlseh)

This shoe is too wide.
Denne sko er for vid.
(dehnneh skoh ehr fohr veed)

This shoe is too narrow.
Denne sko er for snæver.
(dehnneh skoh ehr fohr snehvehr)

These shoes pinch my toes.
Disse sko klemmer mine tæer.
(deesseh skoh klehmmehr maineh tehehr)

I like it.
Den kan jeg lide.
(dehn kahn yeeg leedeh)

I don't like it.
Jeg kan ikke lide den.
(yeeg kahn eekkeh leedeh dehn)

I'll take it.
Jeg tager det.
(yeeg tahgehr day)

I would like a pair of ...
Må jeg bede om et par ...
(mah yeeg beedeh ohm eht pahr)

Do you sell ...?
Sælge De ...?
(sehlgeh dee)

golf shoes with/without spikes:
golfskor med/uden pigge
(golfskohr med/ewdehn peeggeh)

gloves: hansker (handskehr)
hats: hater (hatehr)
light jackets: jakker (yahkkehr)
pants (trousers): bukser (bewksehr)
raincoats: regnfrakker (rehgeenfrahkkehr)

shirts/short/long sleeved:
skjorter/kort/lang ærme
(skyohrtehr/kort/lahng ehrmeh)

shirts with/without a collar/pocket:
skjorter med/uden en krave/lomme
(skyohrtehr med/ewdehn een krahveh/lohmmeh)

sunglasses: solbriller (sohlbreellehr)
sweaters: sweaters (sweaters)
t-shirts: t-shirts (t-shirts)

COLOURS

beige: beige (beige)
black: sort (sohrt)
blue: blå (blaw)
brown: brun (brewn)
cream: cremefarvet (kraymfahrveht)
crimson: højrød (hoyrohd)
gold: guld (gewld)
green: grøn (grurn)
grey: grå (graw)
orange: orange (orahngeh)
pink: lyserød (lewsehrohd)
purple: violet (veeohleht)
red: rød (rohd)
scarlet: skarlagensrød (skahrlahgehnsrohd)
silver: sølv (surl)
turquoise: turkis (tewrkees)
white: hvid (veed)
yellow: gul (gewl)

NUMBERS

```
 0: nul (newl)
 1: en (ehn)
 2: to (too)
 3: tre (tray)
 4: fire (feereh)
 5: fem (fehm)
 6: seks (sayks)
 7: syv (sewv)
 8: otte (ohtteh)
 9: ni (nee)
10: ti (tee)
11: elleve (aylveh)
12: tolv (toal)
13: tretten (traydern)
14: fjorten (fyohrdern)
15: femten (fehmdern)
16: seksten (sayksdern)
17: sytten (sewdern)
18: atten (ahtdern)
19: nitten (needern)
20: tyve (tewver)
21: enogtyve (ehnotewver)
22: toogtyve (too o tewver)
23: treogtyve (tray o tewver)
24: fireogtyve (feerehotewver)
25: femogtyve (fehmotewver)
26: seksogtyve (sayksotewver)
27: syvogtyve (sewvotewver)
28: otteogtyve (ohttehotewver)
29: niogtyve (neeotewver)
30: tredive (traiver)
40: fyrre (fewrrer)
50: halvtreds (hahlvtrays)
60: tres (trays)
70: halvfjerds (hahlvfyayrs)
80: firs (feers)
90: halvfems (hahlvfehms)
100: hundrede (hewndrehdeh)
150: hundrede og halvtreds (hewndrehdeh oh hahlvtrays)
200: to hundrede (too hewndrehdeh)
250: to hundrede og halvtreds (too hewndrehdeh oh hahlvtrays)
```

```
  300: tre hundrede  (tray hewndrehdeh)
  400: fire hundrede  (feereh hewndrehdeh)
  500: fem hundrede  (fehm hewndrehdeh)
  600: seks hundrede  (sayks hewndrehdeh)
  700: syv hundrede  (sewv hewndrehdeh)
  800: otte hundrede  (ohtteh hewndrehdeh)
  900: ni hundrede  (nee hewndrehdeh)
1,000: tusind  (tewseend)

  1st: første  (fohrstehr)
  2nd: anden  (ahnern)
  3rd: tredje  (trayer)
  4th: fjerde  (fyehrer)
  5th: femte  (fehmter)
  6th: sjette  (syayder)
  7th: syvende  (sewverner)
  8th: ottende  (ohttehnder)
  9th: niende  (neeehnder)
 10th: tiende  (teeehnder)
 11th: ellevde  (ehllehvder)
 12th: tolvde  (toalder)
 13th: trettende  (traydernder)
 14th: fjortende  (fyohrdernder)
 15th: femtende  (fehmdernder)
 16th: sekstende  (sayksdernder)
 17th: syttende  (sewdernder)
 18th: attende  (ahtdernder)
```

INTERNATIONAL GOLFERS' LANGUAGE GUIDE

DUTCH

INTERNATIONALE TALEN GIDS VOOR GOLF-SPELERS

NEDERLANDS

'The doctor said "You need exercise, get out and play a round of golf", so here I am.'

BASIC CONVERSATION

Excuse me: Neemt u me niet kwalijk (nehmt ew me nikht kvalaiyk)
Good morning: Goedemorgen (goodehmorgehn)
Good night: Goedenacht (goodehnakht)
Good afternoon: Goedemiddag (goodehmiddahg)
Good bye: Tot ziens (toht zeens)
Good day: Goededag (goodehdahg)
Good evening: Goedenavond (goodehnahovond)
Hello: Hallo (hallo)

I do not speak Dutch.
Ik sprek geen nederlands.
(ik spreek kheen nederlands)

I would like ...
Ik wil graag ... hebben.
(ik vil grahg ... hebben)

I don't understand: Ik begrijp het niet (ik behgraiyp heht nikht)
I understand: Ik begrijp het (ik behgraiyp heht)
No: Nee (nee)
Please: Alstublieft (ahlstewbleeft)

Please bring me ...
Brengt u me ... alstublieft.
(brehngt ew me ... ahlstewbleeft)

Please show me ...
Tonen u me ... alstublieft.
(tohnen ew me ... ahlstewbleeft)

Please give me ...
Geeft u me ... alstublieft.
(geeft ew me ... ahlstewbleeft)

See you later: Tot straks (toht strahks)
See you soon: Tot ziens (toht zeens)
Thank you: Dank u (dahnk ew)
Thank you very much: Hartelijk dank (hahrtehlaiyk dahnk)
That's alright: Niets te danken (nikhts teh dahnken)
Until tomorrow: Tot morgen (toht morgehn)

We would like ...
Wij willen graag ... hebben.
(vee villen grahg ... hebben)

Yes: Ja (ya)
Your welcome: Geen dank (kheen dahnk)

(questions)

Can you give me ...?
Kunt u geeft me?
(kewnt ew geeft me)

Can I have ...?
Mag ik ... hebben?
(mahg ik ... hebben)

Can we have ...?
Mogen wij ... hebben?
(mohgen vee ... hebben)

Can you show me ...?
Kunt u me ... tonen?
(kewnt ew me ... tohnen)

Can you direct me to ...?
Kunt u mij het weg voor ... tonen?
(kewnt ew mee heht vehk voar ... tohnen)

Can you help me please?
Kunt u mij helpen, alstublieft?
(kewnt ew mee hehlpen, ahlstewbleeft)

Can you tell me please?
Kunt u mij zeggen, alstublieft?
(kewnt ew mee zeeggen, ahlstewbleeft)

Do you speak English?
Spreekt u Engels?
(spreekt ew engels)

Do you understand?
Begrijpt u?
(behgraiypt ew)

Is there anyone here who speaks English?
Is er iemand hier die Engels spreekt?
(is ehr eemahnd heer dee engels spreekt)

Is there/are there ...?
is er/zijn er ...?
(is ehr/zaiyn ehr ...)

AT THE GOLF COURSE

No parking.
Verboden te parkeren.
(fehrboden tee parkehen)

May I park here?
Kan ik hier parkeren?
(kahn ik heer parkehren)

Where can I park?
Waar kan ik parkeren?
(vahr kahn ik parkehren)

Straight ahead.
Rechtdoor.
(rekhtdewr)

'We should never have let those rally
drivers into the club.'

To the right.
Links af.
(links ahf)

To the left.
Rechts af.
(rekhts ahf)

Where is the nearest golf course?
Waar is de dichtst bijzijnde golfbaan?
(vahr is dee dikhtst baiyzaiyndeh golfbahn)

Is there another golf course near here?
Is er een andere golfbaan in de buurt?
(is ehr ayn ahndereh golfbahn in dee bewrt)

I would like some information about this course.
Ik zou graag wat informatie over deze baan willen krijgen.
(Ik zow grahk vaht informatee over dezeh bahn villen kraiygehn)

Do you have any course information in English?
Heeft u enige informatie over de golfbaan in het Engels?
(hayft ew ehnikeh informatee over dee golfbahn in het engels)

How much is a round of golf?
Hoeveel kost een rondje golf?
(hoovayl kost ayn rondyeh golf)

How much are the green fees?
Hoewveel bedragen de groene entreegelden?
(hoovayl behdrakehn dee grewneh ehntreekhelden)

What is the fee for 9/18 holes?
Wat moet ik betalen voor negen/achttien holes?
(vaht moat ik behtalehn voar nagehn/ahkhtteen holes)

What is the rate per day/week/month?
Hoeveel kost het per dag/week/maand?
(hoovayl kost heht per dahg/veek/mahnd)

Is there a discount for senior citizens?
Is er korting voor bejaarden?
(is ehr kohrting voar behyahrden)

Is there a discount for children?
Is er korting voor kinderen?
(is ehr kohrting voar kinderehn)

Do I need to be a member?
Moet ik lid zijn?
(moat ik lihd zaiyn)

How much is membership?
Hoeveel kost het lidmaatschap?
(hoovayl kost heht lihdmahtshap)

Per day: per dag (per dahg)
Per week: per week (per veek)
Per month: per maand (per mahnd)
Per year: per jaar (per yahr)

Do I need to make a reservation?
Moet ik van te voren boeken?
(moat ik van teh vorehn bookehn)

I have a reservation.
Ik heb een vaste boeking.
(ik hehb ayn vahsteh booking)

My name is ...
Ik heet ...
(ik heet)

I would like to make a reservation for ...
Ik zou graag willen boeken voor ...
(ik zow grahg villen booken voar)

> myself: mezelf (meezehlf)
> ... people: ... mensen (mehnsen)
> today: vandaag (vandahg)
> this afternoon: vanmiddag (vanmiddahg)
> this evening: vanavond (vanavond)
> tomorrow: morgen (morgehn)
> tomorrow morning: morgen ochtend (morgehn akhtend)
> tomorrow afternoon: morgen middag (morgehn middahg)
> tomorrow evening: morgen avond (morgehn avond)
> next week: volgende week (vohlgendeh veek)
>
> on: op (ohp)
> Monday: maandag (maandahg)
> Tuesday: dinsdag (dinsdahg)
> Wednesday: woensdag (voonsdahg)
> Thursday: donderdag (donderdagh)
> Friday: vrijdag (vraiydahg)
> Saturday: zaterdag (zahterdahg)
> Sunday: zondag (zohndahg)
>
> at: om (ohm)
> one o'clock: een uur (ayn ewr)

one thirty: half twee (half tvae)
two o'clock: twee uur (tvae ewr)
two thirty: half drie (half dree)
three o'clock: drie uur (dree ewr)
three thirty: half vier (half veer)
four o'clock: vier uur (veer ewr)
four thirty: half vijf (half vaiyf)
five o'clock: vijf uur (vaiyf ewr)
five thirty: half zes (half zehs)
six o'clock: zes uur (zehs ewr)
six thirty: half zeven (half zayvehn)
seven o'clock: zeven uur (zayvehn ewr)
seven thirty: half acht (half ahkht)
eight o'clock: acht uur (ahkht ewr)
eight thirty: half negen (half nagehn)
nine o'clock: negen uur (nagehn ewr)
nine thirty: half tien (half teen)
ten o'clock: tien uur (teen ewr)
ten thirty: half elf (half ehlf)
eleven o'clock: elf uur (ehlf ewr)
eleven thirty: half twaalf (half tvahlf)
twelve o'clock: twaalf uur (tvahlf ewr)
twelve thirty: half een (half ayn)
a.m: a.m. (ae em)
p.m: p.m. (pee em)

Please write it down for me.
Schrijf het alstublieft voor mij op.
(shraiyf heht alstewbleeft voar maiy ohp)

What is the dress code for the course?
Welke kleding is vereist op de golfbaan?
(vehlkeh kleeding is vehreest ohp dee golfbahn)

Is there night golfing here?
Kan men hiers avonds golf-spelen?
(kahn men heers avonds golf speelehn)

Are U.S. Golf Association rules and regulations used here?
Worden de regels en bepalingen van de Americaanse Golf
    Association hier gehanteerd?
(vordehn dee regehls een behpahlingen van dee amerikaanseh golf
  assosiation heer gehhanteerd)

Do you accept tee off times?
Wordt er met tee-off tijden gespeeld?
(vohrdt ehr met tee off taiyden gehspeeld)

At what time does the course open/close?
Hoe laat opent/sluit de golfbaan?
(hoh laht opent/slewt dee golfbahn)

Is there a club house here?
Is hier een clubhuis?
(is heer ayn klubhews)

At what time does the club house open/close?
Hoe laat opent/sluit het clubhuis?
(hoh laht opent/slewt heht klubhews)

Is there a pro-shop here?
Is hier een pro-shop?
(is heer ayn pro shop)

At what time does the pro-shop open/close?
Hoe laat opent/sluit de pro-shop?
(hoh laht opent/slewt dee pro shop)

Do you need to be a member to use the club house/pro-shop?
Dient men voor het gebruik van het clubhuis/de pro-shop lid te
    zijn?
(deent men voar heht gehbrewk vahn heht klubhews/dee pro
    shop lihd tee zaiyn)

Is there a putting green/chipping green/driving range?
Is hier een putting/chipping-green/driving range?
(is heer ayn putting/chipping green/driving range)

Is there a practice green?
Is hier een groen oefenveld?
(is heer ayn groehn oyfenvehld)

Can I get a caddie here?
Kan ik hier een caddy krijgen
(kahn ik heer ayn kaddee kraiygen)

What is the going rate for a caddie?
Wat zijn de gangbare kosten voor een caddy?
(vaht zaiyn dee gahngbareh kosten voar ayn kaddee)

Do you have a map of the course?
Heeft u een plattegrond van de baan?
(hayft ew ayn plahttehgrond van dee bahn)

Where is hole ... located?
Waar is hole ...
(vahr is holeh)

Can you show me where the ... is located?
Kunt u mij laten zien waar de ... is?
(kewnt ew mee lahten zeen vahr dee ... is)

    golf club: golfclub (golfklub)
    club house: clubhuis (klubhews)
    pro-shop: pro-shop (pro-shop)

Are spiked shoes required at this course?
Zijn spikes hier op deze baan vereist?
(zaiyn spikes heer ohp dezeh bahn vehraist)

How long is the course?
Hoe lang is de baan?
(hoh lang is dee bahn)

9 hole: negen hole (nagehn holeh)
18 hole: achttien hole (ahkhtteen holeh)

What is the length of this hole?
Wat is de lengte van dit hole?
(vaht is dee lengteh van deet holeh)

What is par for this hole?
Hoeveel par staat voor dit hole?
(hoovayl par staht voar deet holeh)

Is there a residential professional at this course?
Is er een beroeps-speler verbonden aan deze baan?
(is ehr ayn behrewps speelehr vehrbonden ahn dezeh bahn)

What does he/she charge per ½ hour/hour?
Wat berekent hij/zij per half uur/uur?
(vaht behrehkent hee/zee per half ewr/ewr)

PAYING

I would like to pay for ... green fees for ... round(s)/all day.
Ik zou graag willen betalen voor ... groene entreegelden voor ...
    rondje(s)/de hele dag.
(ik zow grahg villen beetahlen voar ... grewneh ehntreegelden voar
    ... rondyeh(s)/dee heleh dagh)

Must I pay in advance?
Moet ik vooruit betalen?
(maot ik vohrewt beetahlen)

May I pay in advance?
Kan ik vooruit betalen?
(kahn ik vohrewt beetahlen)

Must I pay cash?
Moet ik kontant betalen?
(moat ik kontahnt beetahlen)

May I pay by personal cheque?
Kan ik met een betaal-cheque betalen?
(kahn ik meet ayn beetahl check beetahlen)

May I pay with traveller cheques?
Kan ik met reis-cheque betalen?
(kahn ik meet rais-check beetahlen)

May I pay by credit card?
Kan ik met een credit card betalen?
(kahn ik meet ayn kredit kard beetahlen)

Do you accept ...?
Neemt u een ... aan?
(nehmt ew ayn ... ahn)

What will the total cost be?
Hoeveel zal het in totaal kosten?
(hoovayl zahl heht in totahl kohsten)

What is the total cost?
Hoeveel kost het in totaal?
(hoovayl kost heht in totahl)

We would like to pay separately.
Wij zouden graag apart betalen.
(vee zowden grahg apart beetahlen)

I only have large bills.
Ik heb alleen grote rekeningen>
(ik hehb allayn grewteh rehkeningen)

Do you have any change?
Heeft u wisselgeld?
(hayft ew veesselgehld)

I would like some small change.
Ik zou graag wat klein wisselgeld willen hebben.
(ik zow grahg vaht klain veesselgehld villen hehbben)

Who do I make the cheque out to?
Aan wie schrijf ik de cheque uit?
(ahn vee shraiyf ik dee chehk ewt)

Here is my identification.
Hier is mijn identificatie.
(heer is meen identificatee)

bank card: bank pasje   (bahnk pasyeh)
driving licence: rijbewijs (raiybehvaiys)
passport: paspoort   (pahspohrt)

May I have a receipt?
Mag ik een kwitantie hebben?
(mahg ik ayn kveetantee hehbben)

RENTING

I would like to rent ...
Ik zou graag willen huren ...
(ik zow grahg villen hewren)

We would like to rent ...
Wij zouden graag willen huren ...
(vee zowden gragh villen hewren)

How much is it to rent (a) ...?
Hoeveel kost het om (een) te huren ...?
(hoovayl kost heht ohm (ayn) tee hewren)

Where can I rent a/a pair of ...?
Waar kan ik een/paar een huren ...?
(vahr kahn ik ayn/pahr ayn hewren)

> for ½ hour: voor een half uur (voar ayn half ewr)
> for an hour: voor een uur   (voar ayn ewr)
> for a day: voor een dag (voar ayn dahg)

GOLF EQUIPMENT

ball marker(s): ball marker(s) (ball marker(s)
box of golf balls: doos met golf ballen (dohs meet golf ballen)
divot repair tool: divot apparaat (divot ahpparaht)
golf bag: golf-tas (golf tahs)
golf bag umbrella: golf-tas paraplu (golf tahs pahraplew)
golf balls: golf ballen (golf ballen)
golf car: golfwagen (golfvahgen)
golf cart: golfkar (golfkahr)
golf clubs: golf clubs (golf klubs)
golf club cover: golf club bescherming (golf klub behshermeeng)
iron: ijzeren golf club (aiyzehren golf klub)
long iron: lange ijzeren golf club (langeh aiyzehren golf klub)
middle iron: medium ijzeren golf club (medium aiyzehren golf
    klub)
pin: vlag (vlahg)
pitching wedge: pitching wedge (pitching vedj)
putter: putter (putter)
rake: hark (hark)

sand wedge: sand-wedging golf club (sand vedg golf klub)
score card: score-kaart(en) (skohr kahrt(ehn)
shoe spike(s): schoenagel(s) (shohehnahgel(s)
shoe spike tool: schoenagel apparaat (shohehnahgel ahpparaht)
short iron: korte ijzeren golf club (kohrteh aiyzehren golf klub)
tee(s): tee(s) (tee(s)
wedge: wedge (vedj)
wood: houte golf club (howteh golf klub)
wood cover(s): houte bescherming(s) (howteh behshermeeng(s)
wood sock(s): houte bescherming(s) (howteh behshermeeng(s)

CLUBS

1 wood: nummer een hout (newmmer ayn howt)
2 wood: nummer twee hout (newmmer tvae howt)
3 wood: nummer drie hout (newmmer dree howt)
4 wood: nummer vier hout (newmmer veer howt)
5 wood: nummer vijf hout (newmmer vaiyf howt)
6 wood: nummer zes hout (newmmer zehs howt)
7 wood: nummer zeven hout (newmmer zayvehn howt)
8 wood: nummer acht hout (newmmer ahkht howt)
9 wood: nummer negen hout (newmmer nagehn howt)

1 iron: nummer een ijzer (newmmer ayn aiyzehr)
2 iron: nummer twee ijzer (newmmer tvae aiyzehr)
3 iron: nummer drie ijzer (newmmer dree aiyzehr)
4 iron: nummer vier ijzer (newmmer veer aiyzehr)
5 iron: nummer vijf ijzer (newmmer vaiyf aiyzehr)
6 iron: nummer zes ijzer (newmmer zehs aiyzehr)
7 iron: nummer zeven ijzer (newmmer zayvehn aiyzehr)
8 iron: nummer acht ijzer (newmmer ahkht aiyzehr)
9 iron: nummer negen ijzer (newmmer nagehn aiyzehr)

GOLF TERMS

slice: slice (slice)
hook: hook (hook)
Mulligan: mulligan (mulligan)
handicap: handicap (handikap)
double bogey: dubbele bogie (dewbbeleh bogee)
bogey: bogie (bogee)

par: par (pahr)
birdie: birdie (birdee)
eagle: eagle (eegel)
double eagle: dubbele eagle (dewbbeleh eegel)

AT THE PRO-SHOP

I am just looking.
Ik kijk alleen maar rond.
(ik kaiyk allayn mahr rond)

I would like to buy ...
Ik zou graag willen kopen ...
(ik zow grahg villen kohpen)

What size is this?
Welke maat is dit?
(vehlkeh maht is deet)

What size is that?
Welke maat is dat?
(vehlkeh maht is daht)

What size are these?
Welke maat is dit?
(vehlkeh maht is deet)

I would like size ...
Ik zou graag maat ... willen.
(ik zow grahg maht ... villen)

I wear size ...
Ik draag maat ...
(ik drahg maht)

     extra large: extra groot (extra groht)
     large: groot (groht)
     medium: mediium (medium)
     small: small (small)
     extra small: extra small (exta small)
     long: lang (lahng)
     short: kort (kohrt)

regular regular (regular):

This is too large.
Dit is te groot.
(deet is tee groht)

This is too small.
Dit is te klein.
(deet is tee klain)

This is too long.
Dit is te lang.
(det is tee lahng)

This is too short.
Dit is te kort.
(deet is tee kort)

This is good.
Dit is goed.
(deet is good)

It fits very well.
Het past heel goed.
(heht pahst hayl good)

Do you have a larger size?
Heeft u een grotere maat?
(hayft ew ayn grohtereh maht)

Do you have a smaller size?
Heeft u een kleinere maat?
(hayft ew ayn klainereh maht)

Give me the next size up.
Geef mij de volgende grotere maat.
(gayf mee dee vohlgendeh grohtereh maht)

Give me the next size down.
Geef mij de volgende kleinere maat.
(gayf mee de vohlgendeh klainereh maht)

Do you have the same thing in another colour?
Heeft u hetzelfde ding in een andere kleur?
(hayft ew hehtzehlfdeh ding in ayn ahndereh klewr)

May I try this on?
Kan ik dit passen?
(kahn ik deet passen)

Do you have a mirror?
Heeft u een spiegel?
(hayft ew ayn speegel)

Do you have a dressing room?
Heeft u een kleedkamer?
(hayft ew ayn kleedkahmer)

This shoe is too wide.
Deze schoen is te wijd.
(dezeh shohehn is tee vaiyd)

This shoe is too narrow.
Deze schoen is te nauw.
(dezeh shohehn is tee naewv)

These shoes pinch my toes.
Deze schoenen drukken bij de tenen.
(dezeh shohehnen drewkken baiy dee tehnen)

I like it.
Ik vind het leuk.
(ik veend heht lewk)

I don't like it.
Ik vind het niet leuk.
(ik veend heht nikt lewk)

I'll take it.
Ik zal het nemen.
(ik zahl heht nehmen)

I would like a pair of ...
Ik zou graag een paar ... willen.
(ik zow grahg ayn pahr .. villen)

Do you sell ...?
Verkoopt u ...?
(vehrkoopt ew ...)

> golf shoes with/without spikes:
> golf schoenen met/zonder schoennagels
> (golfshohehnen meet/zohnder shohehnnahgels)

> gloves: handschoenen (handshohehnen)
> hats: hoeden (hooden)
> light jackets: lichte jasjes (lishteh yahsyes)
> pants (trousers): pantalons (pantaloons)
> raincoats: regenjas (rehgenyahs)

> shirts/short/long sleeved:
> overhemd/korte/lange mouwen
> (overhehmd/kohrteh/langeh mooven)

> shirts with/without a collar/pocket:
> overhemd met/zonder kraag/zak
> (overhehmd meet/zohnder krahg/zahk)

> sunglasses: zonnebril (zohnnehbreel)
> sweaters: trui (trewee)
> t-shirts: t-shirt (t-shirt)

COLOURS

beige: beige (baygeh)
black: zwart (zvahrt)
blue: blauw (blow)
brown: bruin (brewn)
cream: crème (krehm)
crimson: karmozinnrood (kahrmozaiynroat)
gold: goud (gowd)
green: groen (ghroon)
grey: grijs (graiys)
orange: oranje (ohranyeh)
pink: rose (roseh)
purple: paars (pahrs)
red: rood (roat)
scarlet: scharlakenrood (shahrlakenroat)

silver: zilver (zeelvehr)
turquoise: turkoois (tewrkoys)
white: wit (vit)
yellow: geel (geel)

NUMBERS

0: nul (newl)
1: een (ayn)
2: twee (tvae)
3: drie (dree)
4: vier (veer)
5: vijf (vaiyf)
6: zes (zehs)
7: zeven (zayvehn)
8: acht (ahkht)
9: negen (nagehn)
10: tien (teen)
11: elf (ehlf)
12: twaalf (tvahlf)
13: dertien (dehrteen)
14: viertien (veerteen)
15: vijftien (vaiyfteen)
16: zestien (zehsteen)
17: zeventien (zayvehnteen)
18: achttien (ahkhtteen)
19: negentien (nagehnteen)
20: twintig (tveentig)
21: eenentwintig (ayneentveentig)
22: tweeëntwintig (tvaeyentveentig)
23: drieëntwintig (dreeyentveentig)
24: vierentwintig (veereentveentig)
25: vijfentwintig (vaiyfeentveentig)
26: zesentwintig (zehseentveentig)
27: zevenentwintig (zayvehntveentig)
28: achtentwintig (ahkhttveentig)
29: negenentwintig (nagehntveentig)
30: dertig (dehrtig)
40: veertig (veartig)
50: vijftig (vaiyftig)
60: zestig (zehstig)
70: zeventig (zayuehntig)

```
   80: tachtig (tahkhtig)
   90: negentig (nagehntig)
  100: honderd (hohndert)
  150: honderd vijftig (hohndert vaiyftig)
  200: tweehonderd (tveehohndert)
  250: tweehonderd vijftig (tveehohndert vaiyftig)
  300: driehonderd (dreehohndert)
  400: vierhonderd (veerhohndert)
  500: vijfhonderd (vaiyfhohndert)
  600: zeshonderd (zehshohndert)
  700: zevenhonderd (zayvehnhohndert)
  800: achthonderd (ahkhthohndert)
  900: negenhonderd (nagehnhohndert)
1,000: duizend (dewzent)

  1st: eerste (ehrsteh)
  2nd: tweede (tvaedeh)
  3rd: derde (dehrdeh)
  4th: vierde (veerdeh)
  5th: vijfde (vaiyfdeh)
  6th: zesde (zehsdeh)
  7th: zevende (zayvehndeh)
  8th: achtste (ahkhtsteh)
  9th: negende (nagehndeh)
 10th: tiende (teendeh)
 11th: elfde (ehlfdeh)
 12th: twaalfde (tvahlfdeh)
 13th: dertiende (dehrteendeh)
 14th: veertiende (vearteendeh)
 15th: vijftiende (vaiyfteendeh)
 16th: zestiende (zehsteendeh)
 17th: zeventiende (zayvehnteendeh)
 18th: achttiende (ahkhtteendeh)
```

INTERNATIONAL GOLFERS'
LANGUAGE GUIDE

GERMAN

INTERNATIONALER SPRACHFÜHRER
FÜR GOLFER

DEUTSCH

'Sorry sir, but that doesn't translate.'

here another golf course near here?
t es noch einen Golfplatz hier in der Nähe?
bt ehs nokh ainehn golfplats heer in dehr naeheh)

uld like some information about this course.
hätte gern einige Auskünfte über diesen Golfplatz.
haetteh gern aineegeh aewskewnfteh ewber deesen golfplats)

ou have any course information in English?
n Sie platzinformationen in Englisch?
en zee plats informationehn in english)

uch is a round of golf?
ostet eine Runde Golf?
kohstet aineh rundeh golf)

uch are the green fees?
ch sind die Grüngebühren?
kh sind dee grewngebewhren)

the fee for 9/18 holes?
h ist die Gebühr für neun/achtzehn Löcher?
h eest dee gebewhr fewr noyn/akhttsehn lokher)

he rate per day/week/month?
er Preis pro Tag/Woche/Monat?
t dehr prais pro tahg/vokkeh/mohnaht)

discount for senior citizens?
he Ermässigung für Rentner?
aineh ehrmaessigung fewr rentnehr)

discount for children?
e Ermässigung für Kinder?
aineh ehrmaesseegoong fewr keender)

be a member?
tglied sein?
meetglaid sain)

membership?
t die Mitgliedschaft?
t dee meetglaidshahft)

BASIC CONVERSATION

Excuse me: Entschuldigung (ehntshuldigung)
Good morning: Guten Morgen (gooten mohrgehn)
Good night: Gute Nacht (gooteh nahkt)
Good afternoon: Guten Tag (gooten tahg)
Good bye: Auf Wiedersehen (oof veedersayen)
Good day: Guten Tag (gooten tahg)
Good evening: Guten Abend (gooten ahbent)
Hello: Hallo (hallo)

I do not speak German.
Ich spreche kein Deutsch.
(ish spresheh kain doytch)

I would like ...
Ich möchte
(ish mooshteh)

I don't understand: Ich verstehe nicht (ish fehrstayeh nisht)
I understand: Ich verstehe (ish fehrstayeh)
No: Nein (nain)
Please: Bitte (bitteh)

Please bring me ...
Bitte, Bringen sie mir ...
(bitteh, breengen zee meer)

Please show me ...
Bitte, Zeigen sie mir ...
(bitteh, tsaigen zee meer)

Please give me ...
Bitte, Geben sie mir ...
(bitteh, gehben zee meer)

See you later: Bis später (bis spayter)
See you soon: Bis bald (bis blad)
Thank you: Danke (dankeh)
Thank you very much: Vielen Dank (feelen dank)
That's alright: Gern geschehen (gehrn gehshehen)
Until tomorrow: Bis Morgen (bis mohrgen)

We would like ...
Wir möchten
(veer mooshtehn)

Yes: Ja (ya)
Your welcome: Bitte (bitteh)

(questions)

Can you give me ...?
Können Sie mir ... geben?
(kohnnehn zee meer ... gehben)

Can I have ...?
Kan ich ... haben?
(kahn ish ... hahben)

Can we have ...?
Können wir ... haben?
(kohnnehn veer ... hahben)

Can you show me ...?
Können Sie mir zeigen?
(kohnnehn zee meer tsaigehn)

Can you direct me to ...?
Können Sie mir den Weg Zeigen nach/zu ...?
(kohnnehn zee meer dehn vehg tsaigehn nakh/tsoo)

Can you help me please?
Können Sie mir bitte helfen?
(kohnnehn zee meer hehlfen)

Can you tell me please?
Können Sie mir bitte sagen?
(kohnnehn zee meer bitteh sahgen)

Do you speak English?
Sprechen Sie Englisch?
(spreshen zee English)

Do you understand?
Verstehen Sie?
(vehrstayen zee)

Is there anyone here who speaks English?
Spricht hier jemand Englisch?
(sprisht heer yemand English)

Is there/are there ...?
Gibt es/Gibt es ...?
(geebt ehs/geebt ehs)

AT THE GOLF COURSE

No parking.
Parkverbot
(parkfehrboht)

May I park here?
Darf ich hier parken?
(darf ish heer pahrken)

Where can I park?
Wo kann ich parken?
(voh kahn ish pahrken)

Straight ahead.
geradeaus
(gehrahdaoos)

To the right.
Nach rechts.
(nakh ryehts)

To the left.
Nach links
(nakh links)

Where is the nearest golf course?
Wo ist der nächste Golfplatz?
(voh eest dehr naesteh golfplats)

'I've

Is
Gib
(ge

I wo
Ich
(ish

Do y
Habe
(hahb

How
Was k
(vahs

How m
Wie ho
(vee ho

What is
Wie hoc
(vee hok

What is
Was ist d
(vahs ees

Is there a
Gibt es ei
(geebt ehs

Is there a
Gibt es ein
(geebt ehs

Do I need to
Muss ich M
(mewss ish

How much i
Wieviel koste
(veefeel koste

Per day: Pro Tag (pro tahg)
Per week: Pro Woche (pro vokkeh)
Per month: Pro Monat (pro mohnaht)
Per year: Pro Jahr (pro yahr)

Do I need to make a reservation?
Muss ich vorbestellen?
(mewss ish fohrbeestehllehn)

I have a reservation.
Ich habe eine Vorbestellung.
(ish habeh aineh fohrbestehlloong)

My name is ...
Mein Name ist ...
(main nameh eest)

I would like to make a reservation for ...
Ich möchte eine Vorbestellung für ... machen.
(ish mewsteh aineh fohrbestehlloong fewr ... makhen)

> myself: mich selbst (meesh sehlbst)
> ... people: ... Personen (personehn)
> today: heute (hoyteh)
> this afternoon: heute nachmittag (hoyteh nakhmittahg)
> this evening: heute abend (hoyteh ahbend)
> tomorrow: morgen (mohrgehn)
> tomorrow morning: morgen früh (mohrgehn frewh)
> tomorrow afternoon: morgen nachmittag (mohrgehn nakhmittahg)
> tomorrow evening: morgen abend (mohrgehn ahbend)
> next week: nächste Woche (naekhsteh vokkeh)
>
> on: am (ahm)
> Monday: Montag (mohntahg)
> Tuesday: Dienstag (deenstahg)
> Wednesday: Mittwoch (mittvokh)
> Thursday: Donnerstag (donnerstahg)
> Friday: Freitag (fraitahg)
> Saturday: Samstag/Sonnabend (sahmstahg/sonnahbent)
> Sunday: Sonntag (sohntahg)

at: um (oom)
one o'clock: ein Uhr (ain ewhr)
one thirty: halb zwei (halb tsvai)
two o'clock: zwei Uhr (tsvai ewhr)
two thirty: halb drei (halb dry)
three o'clock: drei Uhr (dry ewhr)
three thirty: halb vier (halb feer)
four o'clock: vier Uhr (feer ewhr)
four thirty: halb fünf (halb fewnf)
five o'clock: fünf Uhr (fewnf ewhr)
five thirty: halb sechs (halb sehks)
six o'clock: sechs Uhr (sehks ewhr)
six thirty: halb sieben (halb seebehn)
seven o'clock: sieben Uhr (seebehn ewhr)
seven thirty: halb acht (halb akht)
eight o'clock: acht Uhr (akht ewhr)
eight thirty: halb neun (halb noyn)
nine o'clock: neun Uhr (noyn ewhr)
nine thirty: halb zehn (halb tsehn)
ten o'clock: zehn Uhr (tsehn ewhr)
ten thirty: halb elf (halb ehlf)
eleven o'clock: elf Uhr (ehlf ewhr)
eleven thirty: halb zwölf (halb tsvolf)
twelve o'clock: zwölf Uhr (tsvolof ewhr)
twelve thirty: halb eins (halb ains)
a.m: vormittag (fohrmittahg)
p.m: nachmittag (nakhmittahg)

Please write it down for me.
Bitte schreiben Sie mir das auf.
(bitteh shraibehn zee meer dahs oof)

What is the dress code for the course?
Welche kleidung trägt man auf dem Golfplatz?
(vehlcheh klaidoong traegt man oof dehm golfplats)

Is there night golfing here?
Gibt es hier Nachtgolf?
(geebt ehs heer nakhtgolf)

Are U.S. Golf Association rules and regulations used here?
Werden die Regeln und Vorschriften des U.S. Golfverbandes hier
    angewendet?
(vehrden dee rehgeln oond fohrshriftehn dehs yew ehs
    golffehrbandehs heer ahngeevehndeht)

Do you accept tee off times?
Akzeptieren Sie Ballabschlagezeiten?
(aktsehpteeren zee ball ahbshlahgeh tsaitehn)

At what time does the course open/close?
Wann öffnet/schliesst der Golfplatz?
(vahn offneht/shleest dehr golfplats)

Is there a club house here?
Gibt es hier ein Klubhaus?
(geebt ehs heer ain klewbhows)

At what time does the club house open/close?
Wann öffnet/schliesst das Klubhaus?
(vahn offneht/shleest dahs klewbhows)

Is there a pro-shop here?
Gibt es hier ein Fachgeschäft?
(geebt ehs heer ain fakhgeshaeft)

At what time does the pro-shop open/close?
Wann öffnet/schliesst das Fachgeschäft?
(vahn offneht/shleest dahs fakhgeshaeft)

Do you need to be a member to use the club house/pro-shop?
Muss man Mitglied sein um das Klubhaus/Fachgeschäft zu
    benutzen?
(mews man meetglaid sain oom dahs klewbhows/fakhgeshaeft
    tsoo benewtsen)

Is there a putting green/chipping green/driving range?
Gibt es einen kleingolfplatz zum putten/ein Chipping Grün/ein
Drivingrange?
(geebt ehs ainen klaingolfplats tsoom pewtten/ain chipping
    grewn/ain driving range)

Is there a practice green?
Gibt es ein Übungsgrün?
(geebt ehs ain ewboongsgrewn)

Can I get a caddie here?
Kann ich hier einen Träger bekommen?
(kahn ish heer ainehn traeger bekommehn)

What is the going rate for a caddie?
Was ist der gegenwärtige Preis für einen Träger?
(vahs eest dehr gehgenwarteegeh prais fewr ainehn traeger)

Do you have a map of the course?
Haben Sie eine Landkarte vom Platz?
(hahben zee aineh landkarteh fom plahts)

Where is hole ... located?
Wo befindet sich loch ...?
(voh befeendeht sish lokh)

Can you show me where the ... is located?
Können Sie mir zeigen wo sich ... befindet?
(kohnnen zee mir tsaigen voh sish ... befeendeht)

> golf club: der Golfklub (dehr golfklub)
> club house: das Klubhaus (dahs klewbhows)
> pro-shop: das Fachgeschäft (dahs fakhgeshaeft)

Are spiked shoes required at this course?
Sind Nagelschuhe auf diesem Platz erforderlich?
(sind nahgelshooheh oof deesehm plahts ehrforderlish)

How long is the course?
Wie gross ist der Platz?
(vee grohss eest dehr plahts)

9 hole: neun Löcher (noyn lokher)
18 hole: achtzehn Löcher (akhttsehn lokher)

What is the length of this hole?
Was ist die Länge dieses Loches?
(vahs eest dee laengeh deesehs lokhehs)

What is par for this hole?
Was ist Pari für dieses Loch?
(vahs eest paree fewr deesehs lokh)

Is there a residential professional at this course?
Gibt es auf diesem Platz einen ansässigen Berufsspieler?
(geebt ehs oof deesehm plahts ainehn ansaesseegehn
  behroofsspeelehr)

What does he/she charge per ½ hour/hour?
Was sind seine/ihre Gebühren für eine halb stunde/stunde?
(vahs seend saineh/eehreh gebewhrehn fewr aineh halb stundeh/
  stundeh)

PAYING

I would like to pay for ... green fees for ... round(s)/all day.
Ich möchte ... Grüngebühren für ... Runde(n)/den ganzen Tag
  bezahlen.
(ish mewsteh ... grewngehbewhrehn fewr ... roondeh(n)/dehn
  gantsehn tahg behtsahlehn)

Must I pay in advance?
Muss ich im voraus bezahlen?
(mewss ish eem fohroos behtsahlehn)

May I pay in advance?
Darf ich im voraus bezahlen?
(darf ish eem fohroos behtsahlehn)

Must I pay cash?
Muss ich bar bezahlen?
(mewss ish bahr behtsahlehn)

May I pay by personal cheque?
Darf ich mit einem personlichen Scheck bezahlen?
(darf ish meet ainehm personlishehn shekh behtsahlehn)

May I pay with traveller cheques?
Darf ich mit Reisescheck bezahlen?
(darf ish meet raisehshekh behtsahlehn)

May I pay by credit card?
Darf ich mit Kreditkarte bezahlen?
(darf ish met kreditkarteh behtsahlehn)

Do you accept ...?
Nehmen Sie ...?
(nehmen zee ...)

What will the total cost be?
Wie hoch wird der Gesamtbetrag sein?
(vee hokh veerd dehr gesahmtbehtrag sain)

What is the total cost?
Wie hoch ist der Gesamtbetrag?
(vee hokh eest dehr gesahmtbehtrag)

We would like to pay separately.
Wir möchten getrennt bezahlen
(veer mooshtehn gehtrehnnt behtsahlehn)

I only have large bills.
Ich habe nur grosse Scheine.
(ish hahbeh newr grosseh shaineh)

Do you have any change?
Haben Sie Wechselgeld?
(hahben zee vekhsehlgehld)

I would like some small change.
Ich möchte gern etwas Kleingeld.
(ish mooshteh gehrn ehtvahs klaingehld)

Who do I make the cheque out to?
Auf wen schreibe ich den Scheck aus?
(oof vehn shraibeh ish dehn shekh oos)

Here is my identification.
Hier ist meine Identifikation.
(heer eest maineh aidehnteefeekateeohn)

bank card: Bank Karte (bahnk karteh)
driving licence: Führerschein (fewhrehrshain)
passport: Pass (pahss)

May I have a receipt?
Darf ich eine Quittung haben?
(darf ish aineh kwittoong hahben)

RENTING

I would like to rent ...
Ich möchte ... mieten.
(ish mooshteh ... meetehn)

We would like to rent ...
Wir möchten ... mieten.
(veer mooshtehn ... meetehn)

How much is it to rent (a) ...?
Wieviel kostet es (ein/e/en) ... zu mieten?
(veefeel kosteht ehs (ain/eh/ehn) ... tsoo meetehn)

Where can I rent a/a pair of ...?
Wo kan ich eine/paar ein/e ... mieten?
(voh kahn ish aineh/paar ain/eh ... meetehn)

>   for ½ hour: für eine halbe stunde (fewr aineh halbeh
>   stundeh)
>   for an hour: für eine stunde (fewr aineh stundeh)
>   for a day: für einen Tag (fewr ainehn tahg)

GOLF EQUIPMENT

ball marker(s): Ballmarkierung(en) (ballmarkeeroong(en))
box of golf balls: Schachtel Golfbälle (shakhtehl golfbaelleh)
divot repair tool: Reparaturwerkzeug fürs Grün (reparatoorvehrk
tsoig fewrs grewhn)
golf bag: Golftasche (golftasheh)
golf bag umbrella: Golftaschenschirm (golftashensheerm)
golf balls: Golfbälle (golfbaelleh)
golf car: Golfwagen (golfvahgen)
golf cart: Golfkarren (golfkahrren)
golf clubs: Golfschläger (golfshlaegehr)
golf club cover: Golfschläger-überzug (golfshlaegehr-ewbertsoog)
iron: eiserner Golfschläger (aisehrnehr golfshlaeger)

long iron: langer eiserner Golfschläger (lahnger aisehrnehr
    golfshlaeger)
middle iron: mittlerer eiserner Golfschläger (mittlehrehr
    aisehrnehr golfshlaeger)
pin: Fahne (fahneh)
pitching wedge: Golfschläger zum Pitchen (golfshlaeger tsoom
    pitchen)
putter: Putter (pewtter)
rake: Harke (harkeh)
sand wedge: Golfschläger für Sand (golfshlaeger fewr sand)
score card: Punktekarte (poonkehkarteh)
shoe spike(s): Schuhnagel(Schuhnägel)
    (shoohnahgel(shoohnaegel)
shoe spike tool: Werkzeug für Schuhnägel (vehrktsoig fewrs
    shoohnaegel)
short iron: kurzerer Golfschläger (koortsehrehr golfshlaeger)
tee(s): Abschlagstelle(n) (ahbshlahgstehllen)
wedge: Golfschläger zum pitchen (golfshlaeger tsoom pitchen)
wood: holzer Golfschläger (holtsehr golfshlaeger)
wood cover(s): holzer Golfschläger-überzug (holtsehr
    golfshlaeger-ewbertsoog)
wood sock(s): Golfsock(en) für holzer Golfschläger (sohk(ehn)
    fewr holtsehr golfshlaeger)

CLUBS

1 wood: nummer eins Holz (noommehr ains holts)
2 wood: nummer zwei Holz (noommehr tsvai holts)
3 wood: nummer drei Holz (noommehr dry holts)
4 wood: nummer vier Holz (noommehr feer holts)
5 wood: nummer fünf Holz (noommehr fewnf holts)
6 wood: nummer sechs Holz (noommehr sekhs holts)
7 wood: nummer sieben Holz (noommehr seebehn holts)
8 wood: nummer acht Holz (noommehr akht holts)
9 wood: nummer neun Holz (noommehr noyn holts)

1 iron: nummer eins Eisen (noommehr ains aisehn)
2 iron: nummer zwei Eisen (noommehr tsvai aisehn)
3 iron: nummer drei Eisen (noommehr dry aisehn)
4 iron: nummer vier Eisen (noommehr feer aisehn)
5 iron: nummer fünf Eisen (noommehr fewnf aisehn)
6 iron: nummer sechs Eisen (noommehr sekhs aisehn)

7 iron: nummer sieben Eisen (noommehr seebehn aisehn)
8 iron: nummer acht Eisen (noommehr akht aisehn)
9 iron: nummer neun Eisen (noommehr noyn aisehn)

GOLF TERMS

slice: Slice (slais)
hook: Hook (hook)
Mulligan: Mulligan (mulligan)
handicap: Handikap (handikap)
double bogey: Doppelter Bogie (doppehltehr bogee)
bogey: Bogie (bogee)
par: Pari (paree)
birdie: Birdie (birdee)
eagle: Eagle (eegel)
double eagle: Doppelter Eagle (doppehltehr eegel)

AT THE PRO-SHOP

I am just looking.
Ich Schaue mich nur um.
(ish shaeweh mish newr oom)

I would like to buy ...
Ich möchte ... kaufen.
(ish mooshteh .. kaewfehn)

What size is this?
Welche Grösse ist dies?
(vehlcheh grosseh eest dees)

What size is that?
Welche Grösse ist das?
(vehlcheh grosseh eest das)

What size are these?
Welche Grösse sind diese?
(vehlcheh grosseh sind deeseh)

I would like size ...
Ich möchte Grösse ...
(ish mooshteh grosseh)

I wear size ...
Ich träge Grösse ...
(ish trageh grosseh)

> extra large: extra gross (extra gross)
> large: gross (gross)
> medium: mittel (mittel)
> small: klein (klain)
> extra small: extra klein (extra klain)
> long: lang (lahng)
> short: kurz (koorts)
> regular: regular (regular)

This is too large.
Dies ist zu gross.
(dees eest tsoo gross)

This is too small.
Dies ist zu klein.
(dees eest tsoo klain)

This is too long.
Dies ist zu lang.
(dees eest tsoo lahng)

This is too short.
Dies ist zu kurz.
(dees eest tsoo koorts)

This is good.
Das ist gut.
(dahs eest goot)

'How would you manage without your "Do you speak golf?"

It fits very well.
Es passt sehr gut.
(ehs pahsst sehr goot)

Do you have a larger size?
Haben Sie eine grössere Grösse?
(haben zee aineh grossehreh grosseh)

Do you have a smaller size?
Haben Sie eine kleinere Grösse?
(haben zee aineh klainehreh grosseh)

Give me the next size up.
Geben Sie mir die Nächstgrössere Grösse.
(gehben zee meer dee naestrossehreh grosseh)

Give me the next size down.
Geben Sie mir die Nächstkleinere Grösse.
(gehben zee meer dee naestklainehreh grosseh)

Do you have the same thing in another colour?
Haben Sie dasselbe in einer anderen Farbe?
(haben zee dassehlbeh in ainehr andehren fahrbeh)

May I try this on?
Darf ich das anprobieren?
(darf ish dahs anprobeerehn)

Do you have a mirror?
Haben Sie einen Speigel?
(haben zee ainehn speegehl)

Do you have a dressing room?
Haben Sie eine Umkleidekabine?
(haben zee aineh oomklaidehkabineh)

This shoe is too wide.
Dieser Schuh ist zu weit.
(deesehr shooh eest tsoo vait)

This shoe is too narrow.
Dieser Schuh ist zu eng.
(deesehr shooh eest tsoo eng)

These shoes pinch my toes.
Diese Schuhe drücken meine Zehen.
(deeseh shooheh drewkken maineh tsehehn)

I like it.
Es gefällt mir.
(ehs gefaellt meer)

I don't like it.
Es gefällt mir nicht.
(ehs gefaellt meer nisht)

I'll take it.
Ich nehme es.
(ish nehmeh ehs)

I would like a pair of ...
Ich möchte ein Paar ...
(ish mooshteh ain paar)

Do you sell ...?
Verkaufen Sie ...?
(fehrkaewfehn zee)

> golf shoes with/without spikes:
> Golfschuhe/mit/ohne Nägel
> (golfshooheh/meet/ohneh naegel)

> gloves: Handshuhe (handshooheh)
> hats: Hüte (hooteh)
> light jackets: leichte Jacken (laishteh yakkehn)
> pants (trousers): Hosen (hohsehn)
> raincoats: Regenmäntel (rehgehnmaentehl)

> shirts/short/long sleeved:
> Hemden/kurz/langärmelig
> (hemdehn/koorts/lahngaermehleeg)

> shirts with/without a collar/pocket:
> Hemd mit/ohne Kragen/Tasche
> (hehmd meet/ohneh krahgen/tasheh)

> sunglasses: Sonnenbrillen (sohnehnbrillehn)
> sweaters: Pullover (pullover)
> t-shirts: T-Hemd (t-hehmd)

COLOURS

beige: beige (baygeh)
black: schwarz (shvarts)
blue: blau (blaew)
brown: braun (braewn)
cream: Cremefarbe (kreemehfarbeh)
crimson: leuchtend rot (loochtenhd roht)
gold: golden (golden)
green: grün (grewn)
grey: grau (graew)
orange: orange (orangeh)
pink: rosa (rosah)
purple: violett (fiolett)
red: rot (roht)
scarlet: scharlachrot (sharlakhroht)
silver: silbern (silbern)
turquoise: türkisfarben (toorkishfarbeh)
white: weiss (vais)
yellow: gelb (gelb)

NUMBERS

0: null (nool)
1: eins (ains)
2: zwei (tsvai)
3: drei (dry)
4: vier (feer)
5: fünf (fewnf)
6: sechs (sekhs)
7: sieben (seebehn)
8: acht (akht)
9: neun (noyn)
10: zehn (tsehn)
11: elf (ehlf)
12: zwölf (tsvolf)
13: dreizehn (drytsehn)
14: vierzehn (feertsehn)
15: fünfzehn (fewnftsehn)
16: sechzehn (sekhstsehn)
17: siebzehn (seebtsehn)
18: achtzehn (akhttsehn)

19: neunzehn (noyntsehn)
20: zwanzig (tsvantsig)
21: einundzwanzig (ainoondtsvantsig)
22: zweiundzwanzig (tsvaioondtsvantsig)
23: dreiundzwanzig (dryoondtsvantsig)
24: vierundzwanzig (feeroondtsvantsig)
25: fünfundzwanzig (fewnfoondtsvantsig)
26: sechsundzwanzig (sekhsoondtsvantsig)
27: siebenundzwanzig (seebehnoondtsvantsig)
28: achtundzwanzig (akhtoondtsvantig)
29: neunundzwanzig (noynoondtsvantsig)
30: dreissig (drytsig)
40: vierzig (feertsig)
50: fünfzig (fewnftsig)
60: sechzig (sekhtsig)
70: siebzig (seebtsig)
80: achtzig (akhttsig)
90: neunzig (noyntsig)
100: hundert (hundert)
150: hundertfünfzig (hundertfewnftsig)
200: zweihundert (tsvaihundert)
250: zweihundertfünfzig (tsvaihundertfewnftsig)
300: dreihundert (dryhundert)
400: vierhundert (feerhunder)
500: fünfhundert (fewnfhundert)
600: sechshundert (sekhshundert)
700: siebenhundert (seebehnhundert)
800: achthundert (akhthundert)
900: neunhundert (noynhundert)
1,000: tausend (taewsend)

1st: erste (ehrsteh)
2nd: zweite (tsvaiteh)
3rd: dritte (dritteh)
4th: vierte (feerteh)
5th: fünfte (fewnfteh)
6th: sechste (sekhsteh)
7th: siebte (seebteh)
8th: achte (akhteh)
9th: neunte (noynteh)
10th: zehnte (tsehnteh)
11th: elfte (ehlfteh)
12th: zwölfte (tsvolfteh)

13th: dreizehnte (drytsehnteh)
14th: vierzehnte (feertsehnteh)
15th: fünfzehnte (fewnftsehnteh)
16th: sechzehnte (sekhtsehnteh)
17th: siebzehnte (seebtsehnteh)
18th: achtzehnte (akhttsehnteh)

INTERNATIONAL GOLFERS'
LANGUAGE GUIDE

FRENCH

GUIDE DE VOCABULAIRE
INTERNATIONAL DES GOLFEURS

FRANÇAIS

'EAU!'

BASIC CONVERSATION

Excuse me: Excusez-moi (ehkskewzay mwah)
Good morning: Bonjour (bawnzhewr)
Good night: Bonne nuit (bawnnwee)
Good afternoon: Bonjour (bawnzhewr)
Good bye: Au revoir (oh rervwahr)
Good day: Bonjour (bawnzhewr)
Good evening: Bonsoir (bawnswahr)
Hello: Âllo (ahlloh)

I do not speak French.
Je ne parle pas Français.
(zheh neh pahrl pah frahnsay)

I would like ...
Je voudrais ...
(zheh vewdray)

I don't understand: Je ne comprends pas. (zheh neh komprehn
pah)
I understand: Je comprends. (zheh komprehn)
No: non (noh)
Please: S'il vous plaît (seel vew pleh)

Please bring me ...
S'il vous plaît apportez-moi ...
(seel vew pleh ahpohrtay mwah)

Please show me ...
S'il vous plaît montrez-moi ...
(seel vew pleh mohntray mwah)

Please give me ...
S'il vous plaît donnez-moi ...
(seel vew pleh dohnnay mwah)

See you later: À plus tard. (ah plews tahrd)
See you soon: À bientôt. (ah beentoh)
Thank you: Merci (mersee)
Thank you very much: Merci beaucoup. (mersee bewkew)
That's alright: Il n'y a pas de quoi. (eel nee ah pah dee kwah)
Until tomorrow: À demain. (ah deemahn)

We would like ...
Nous voudrions ...
(new vewdreeohn)

Yes: Oui (wee)
Your welcome: De rien (dee reahn)

(questions)

Can you give me ...?
Pouvez-vous donnez-moi ...?
(pewvay-vew dohnneh-mwah)

Can I have ...?
Puis-je avoir ...?
(pew zhew ahvwahr)

Can we have ...?
Pouvons-nous avoir ...?
(pewvohn-new ahvwahr)

Can you show me ...?
Pouvez-vous m'indiquer ...?
(pewvay vew meendeekey)

Can you direct me to ...?
Pouvez-vous m'indiquer la direction de ...?
(pewvay-vew meendeekey lah deerektiyon deh)

Can you help me please?
Pouvez-vous m'aider s'il vous plaît?
(pewvay-vew meeaedehr seel vew pleh)

Can you tell me please?
Pouvez-vous me dire s'il vous plaît?
(pewvay-vew mee deer seel vew pleh)

Do you speak English?
Parlez-vous anglais?
(pahrlay-vew ahnglay)

Do you understand?
Comprenez-vous?
(komprehnay-vew)

Is there anyone here who speaks English?
Y-a-t-il quelqu'un qui parle anglais ici?
(ee-ah-teel kewlkewn kee pahrl ahnglay eesee)

Is there/are there ...?
Y-a-t-il/y-a-t-il?
(ee-ah-teel/ee-ah-teel)

AT THE GOLF COURSE

No parking.
Parking interdit
(parkeeng eentehrdee)

May I park here?
Puis-je me garer ici?
(pews-zheh mee gahreh eesee)

Where can I park?
Où puis-je me garer?
(ew pew-zheh mee gahreh)

Straight ahead.
Tout droit
(too drewaht)

To the right.
à droite.
(ah drewaht)

To the left.
à gauche.
(ah gohsh)

'If that's the spawn, heaven help us
when they hatch out.'

Where is the nearest golf course?
Où se trouve le terrain de golf le plus proche?
(ew say trewv leh tehrrayn deh golf leh plews prohs)

Is there another golf course near here?
Existe-t-il un autre terrain de golf près d'ici?
(ekseeteh-teel ewn ohtreh tehrrayn deh golf pray deesee)

I would like some information about this course.
J'aimerais des informations sur ce parcours.
(zhaymehray deh informatiyon sewr seh pahrkowr)

Do you have any course information in English?
Avez-vous des informations en anglais sur le parcours?
(ahvay-vew deh informatiyon ehn ahngay sewr leh pahrkowr)

How much is a round of golf?
Combien coûte une partie de golf?
(kohmbeahn kohteh ewn pahrtee deh golf)

How much are the green fees?
A combien s'élèvent les droits d'entrée?
(ah kohmbeahn seelevehn leh drewaht deentree)

What is the fee for 9/18 holes?
Quel est le tarif pour neuf/dix-huit trous?
(keel eh leh tahreef pohr newf/dees-weet trew)

What is the rate per day/week/month?
Quel est le tarif journalier/hebdomadaire/mensuel?
(keel eh leh tahreef zhyurnalee/ehbdohmadeer/mehnsewl)

Is there a discount for senior citizens?
Y-a-t-il une réduction pour les personnes du troisième Âge?
(ee-ah-teel ewn reeduktiyon pohr leh persohn dew trawseem ahzh)

Is there a discount for children?
Y-a-t-il une réduction pour les enfants?
(ee-ah-teel ewn reeduktiyon pohr leh ehnfahnt)

Do I need to be a member?
Est-il nécessaire d'être membre?
(ehs-eel nehsessaree dehtreh mehmbr)

How much is membership?
A combien se montre la cotisation?
(ah kohmbeahn say mohntree lah kohteesatiyon)

Per day: pour un jour (pohr ewn zhewr)
Per week: pour une semaine (pohr ewn seemahn)
Per month: pour un mois (pohr ewn mawh)
Per year: pour un an (pohr ewn ahn)

Do I need to make a reservation?
Dois-je réserver?
(daw-zheh reeservee)

I have a reservation.
J'ai réservé.
(zhae rehseervee)

My name is ...
Je m'appelle ...
(zheh mahppehll)

I would like to make a reservation for ...
J'aimerais faire une réservation pour ...
(zhaemehray faer ewn rehsehrvateeohn pohr)

> myself: moi-même (mawh mehm)
> ... people: ... personnes (pehrsohnn)
> today: aujourd'hui (ahzhewrdwee)
> this afternoon: cette après-midi (sehtt ahprae-meedee)
> this evening: ce soir (seh swahr)
> tomorrow: demain (deemahn)
> tomorrow morning: demain matin (deemahn mahtehn)
> tomorrow afternoon: demain après-midi (deemahn ahprae-meedee)
> tomorrow evening: demain soir (deemahn swahr)
> next week: la semaine prochaine (lah seemahn prohchahn)
>
> on: pour le (pohr leh)
> Monday: lundi (lewndee)
> Tuesday: mardi (mahrdee)
> Wednesday: mercredi (mehrkrerdee)
> Thursday: jeudi (zhewdee)
> Friday: vendredi (vahndredee)
> Saturday: samedi (sahmehdee)
> Sunday: dimanche (deemahnch)

at: à (ah)
one o'clock: une heure (ewn ewhr)
one thirty: une heure et demie (ewn ewhr eh dehmee)
two o'clock: deux heures (dew ewhr)
two thirty: deux heures et demie (dew ewhr eh dehmee)
three o'clock: trois heures (traw ewhr)
three thirty: trois hueres et demie (traw ewhr eh dehmee)
four o'clock: quatre heures (kahtr ewhr)
four thirty: quatre heures et demie (kahtr ewhr eh dehmee)
five o'clock: cinq heures (sahnk ewhr)
five thirty: cinq heures et demie (sahnk ewhr eh dehmee)
six o'clock: six heures (sees ewhr)
six thirty: six heures et demie (sees ewhr eh dehmee)
seven o'clock: sept heures (seht ewhr)
seven thirty: sept heures et demie (seht ewhr eh dehmee)
eight o'clock: huit heures (weet ewhrs)
eight thirty: huit heures et demie (weet ewhr eh dehmee)
nine o'clock: neuf heures (newf ewhr)
nine thirty: neuf heures et demie (newf ewhr eh dehmee)
ten o'clock: dix heures (dees ewhr)
ten thirty: dix heures et demie (dees ewhr eh dehmee)
eleven o'clock: onze heures (ohnz ewhr)
eleven thirty: onze heures et demie (hnz ewhr eh dehmee)
twelve o'clock: midi (meedee)
twelve thirty: midi et dimi (meedee eh deemee)
a.m: du matin (dew mahtan)
p.m: de l'après-midi (deh lahprae-meedee)

Please write it down for me.
Pouvez-vous me l'écrire s'il vous plaît.
(pewvay-vew mee lehsreer seel vew pleh)

What is the dress code for the course?
Quelle est la tenue à porter au terrain de golf?
(kwehll eh lah teenew ah pohrtehr aew terraen deh golf)

Is there night golfing here?
Est-il possible ici de jouer au golf la nuit?
(ehs-eel posseebl eesee deh johay aew golf lah neweet)

Are U.S. Golf Association rules and regulations used here?
La réglementation de l'Association de Golf américaine est-elle
    utilisée ici?
(lah rehgleemehntahteeohn deh lahssoseeateeohn deh golf
    ahmehrikahn ehs-ehl ewteeleesay eesee)

Do you accept tee off times?
Acceptez-vous les temps de début de frappe de la balle?
(aksehptay-vew leh tehmps deh dehbew dee frahpp deh lah bahll)

At what time does the course open/close?
Quelles sont les heures d'ouverture/de fermeture du golf?
(kwehll sohnt leh ewhr dohvehrtewr/deh fehrmehtewr dew golf)

Is there a club house here?
Y-a-t-il un chalet ici?
(ee-ah-teel ewn chahlay eesee)

At what time does the club house open/close?
A quelle heure ouvre/ferme la chalet?
(ah kehll ewhr ohvehr/fehrm lah chahlay)

Is there a pro-shop here?
Y-a-t-il une boutique spécialisée ici?
(ee-ah-teel ewn bewteek spehseealeesay eesee)

At what time does the pro-shop open/close?
A quelle heure ouvre/ferme la boutique spécialisée?
(ah kehll ewhr ohvehr/fehrm lah bewteek spehseealeesay)

Do you need to be a member to use the club house/pro-shop?
Faut-il être membre pour pouvoir utiliser le chalet/la boutique
    spécialisée?
(faeteel ehtreh mehmbr pohr pewvohr ewteeleesay leh chahlay/lah
    bewteek spehseealseesay)

Is there a putting green/chipping green/driving range?
Y-a-t-il un green de putting/green d'approche/green longue
    distance?
(ee-ah-teel ewn green deh putting/green dahpproch/green lohng
    distance)

Is there a practice green?
Y-a-t-il un green d'entraînement?
(ee-ah-teel ewn green dehntraenehment)

Can I get a caddie here?
Puis-je louer un caddie ici?
(pews-zheh lewehr ewn kaddee eesee)

What is the going rate for a caddie?
A combien se louent les caddies ici?
(ah kohmbeahn say leuehnt leh kaddee eesee)

Do you have a map of the course?
Avez-vous une carte du parcours?
(ahvay vew ewn kahrt dew pahrkohrs)

Where is hole ... located?
Où se situe le trou ...?
(ew say seeteway leh troh)

Can you show me where the ... is located?
Pouvez-vous m'indiquer où se trouve ...?
(pewvay-vew meendeekehr ew say trewv)

> golf club: le club de golf (leh klewb dee golf)
> club house: le chalet (leh chahlay)
> pro-shop: la boutique spécialisée (lah bewteek
>   spehssealseesay)

Are spiked shoes required at this course?
Faut-il porter des chaussures cloutées sur ce terrain?
(faet eel pohrtehr dehs chawssewr clohtay sewr seh tehrraen)

How long is the course?
Quelle est la longueur du parcours?
(kehll eh lah lohngewr dew pahrkohr)

9 hole: neuf trous (newf troh)
18 hole: dix-huit trous (dees-weet troh)

What is the length of this hole?
Quelle est la distance de ce trou?
(kehll eh lah deestahns deh seh troh)

What is par for this hole?
Quelle est la normale pour ce trou?
(kehll eh lah nohrmahl pohr seh troh)

Is there a residential professional at this course?
Est-il possible de louer les services d'un instructeur à ce golf?
(ehst-eel pohsseebl deh lewehr leh servees dewn eenstrewtewr ah
    seh golf)

What does he/she charge per ½ hour/hour?
Quels sont ses tarifs pour trente minuntes/une heure?
(kewl sohnt sehs tahreef pohr trehnt meenewt/ewn ewhr)

PAYING

I would like to pay for ... green fees for ... round(s)/all day.
Je voudrais payer pour ... droits d'entrée pour ... partie(s)/toute la
    journée.
(zheh vewdray payeh pohr... droht dehntree pohr ... pahrtee(s)/
    tew lah zhohrnee)

Must I pay in advance?
Dois-je payer à l'avance?
(daw zheh payeh ah lahvahns)

May I pay in advance?
Puis-je payer à l'avance?
(pews-zheh payeh ah lahvahns)

Must I pay cash?
Dois-je payer en liquide?
(daw zheh payeh ehn leekeweed)

May I pay by personal cheque?
Puis-je payer par chèque?
(pews zheh payeh pahr check)

May I pay with traveller cheques?
Puis-je payer par chèque de voyage?
(pews zheh payeh pahr check deh voyahj)

May I pay by credit card?
Puis-je payer par carte de crédit?
(pews zheh payeh pahr kahrt deh krehdeet)

Do you accept ...?
Acceptez-vous ...?
(aksehptay vew ...)

What will the total cost be?
A combien se montera le total?
(ah kohmbeahn say mohntehrah leh tohtahl)

What is the total cost?
Quel est le montant total?
(kewl eh leh mohntant tohtahl)

We would like to pay separately.
Nous aimerions payer séparément.
(news ahmehreeohns payeh sehpahrehmehnt)

I only have large bills.
Je n'ai que des grosses coupures.
(zheh nae kee deh grohsseh kohpewr)

Do you have any change?
Auriez-vous de la monnaie?
(awray vew deh lah mohnnay)

I would like some small change.
J'aimerais un peu de petite monnaie.
(zheh ahmehray ewn pew deh pehteet mohnnay)

Who do I make the cheque out to?
A quel nom dois-je faire le chèque?
(ah kewl nohm daw zheh faer leh check)

Here is my identification.
Voici ma pièce d'identité.
(voysee mah pees deedehnteeteh)

bank card: carte bancaire (kahrt bahnkair)
driving licence: permis de conduire (pehrmee deh kohndewr)
passport: passeport (pahsspohrt)

May I have a receipt?
Puis-je avoir un reçu?
(pews zheh ahvohr ewn rehsew)

RENTING

I would like to rent ...
J'aimerais louer ...
(zhehahmehray lewehr)

We would like to rent ...
Nous aimerions louer ...
(news ahmehreeohns lewehr)

How much is it to rent (a) ...?
A combien se monte la location (d'un)
(ah kohmbeahn say mohnt lah location (dewn)

Where can I rent a/a pair of ...?
Où puis-je louer une/une paire de...?
(ew pews zheh lewehr ewn/ewn paer deh)

> for ½ hour: pour une demi-heure (pohr ewn dehmee hewr)
> for an hour: pour une heure (pohr ewn hewr)
> for a day: pour la journée (pohr lah zhohrnee)

GOLF EQUIPMENT

ball marker(s): marqueur(s) de balle (markewr(s) deh bahll)
box of golf balls: boîte de balles de golf (bewaht deh bahll deh golf)
divot repair tool: outil de réparation de mottes de gazon (ohteel deh rehpahrahteeon deh mohtt deh gahzohn)
golf bag: sac de golf (sahk deh golf)
golf bag umbrella: parapluie pour sac de golf (pahraplew pohr sahk deh golf)
golf balls: balles de golf (bahll deh golf)
golf car: voiturette de golf (vohtewrehtt deh golf)
golf cart: chariot de golf (chahreeoht deh golf)
golf clubs: clubs de golf (klewb deh golf)

golf club cover: étui pour club de golf (ehtewee pohr klewb deh golf)
iron: fer (fehr)
long iron: fer long (fehr lohng)
middle iron: fer moyen (fehr moyehn)
pin: drapeau de trou (drahpeaw deh troh)
pitching wedge: cocheur d'allée (kohchehr dahllay)
putter: fer droit (fehr drahwt)
rake: rateau (rahtoh)
sand wedge: cocheur de sable (kohchehr deh sahbl)
score card: feche de marquage des points (feech deh markazh deh points)
shoe spike(s): clou(s) pour chaussures (kloh(s) pohr chohssewr)
shoe spike tool: outil pour des chaussures avec clous (ohteel pohr deh chohssewrs ahvehk kloh)
short iron: fer court (fehr kohrt)
tee(s): tee(s) (tee(s))
wedge: cocheur d'allée (kohchehr dahllay)
wood: bois (bewah)
wood cover(s): étui pour club de bois (ehtewee pohr klewb deh bewah)
wood sock(s): étui pour club de bois (ehtewee pohr klewb deh bewah)

CLUBS

1 wood: bois une (bewah ewn)
2 wood: bois deux (bewah dew)
3 wood: bois trois (bewah traw)
4 wood: bois quatre (bewah kahtr)
5 wood: bois cinq (bewah sahnk)
6 wood: bois six (bewah sees)
7 wood: bois sept (bewah seht)
8 wood: bois huit (bewah weet)
9 wood: bois neuf (bewah newf)

1 iron: fer une (fehr ewn)
2 iron: fer deux (fehr dew)
3 iron: fer troix (fehr traw)
4 iron: fer quatre (fehr kahtr)
5 iron: fer cinq (fehr sahnk)
6 iron: fer six (fehr sees)

7 iron: fer sept (fehr seht)
8 iron: fer huit (fehr weet)
9 iron: fer neuf (fehr newf)

GOLF TERMS

slice: slice (slais)
hook: coup hook (koo hook)
Mulligan: mulligan (mulligan)
handicap: handicap (handikap)
double bogey: double bogee (doobel bogee)
bogey: bogee (bohgee)
par: par (par)
birdie: birdie (birdee)
eagle: eagle (eegel)
double eagle: double eagle (doobel eegel)

AT THE PRO-SHOP

I am just looking.
Je regarde seulement.
(zheh reegahrd sewlehment)

I would like to buy ...
J'aimerais acheter.
(zhehahmehray ahchehtay)

What size is this?
Ceci fait quelle taille?
(sehsee fayt kwehl tahll)

What size is that?
Cela fait quelle taille?
(sehlah fayt kwehl tahll)

What size are these?
Celles-ci font quelle taille?
(sehlleh-see fohn kwehl tahll)

I would like size ...
J'aimerais la taille ...
(zhehahmehray lah tahll)

I wear size ...
Je fais du ...
(zheh fay dew)

> extra large: extra large (extra lahrzh)
> large: grand (grahnd)
> medium: moyen (moyehn)
> small: petit (pehteet)
> extra small: extra petit (extra pehteet)
> long: long (lohng)
> short: court (kohrt)
> regular: regular (regular)

This is too large.
Ceci est trop grand.
(sehsee eh troh grahnd)

This is too small.
Ceci est trop petit.
(sehsee eh troh pehteet)

This is too long.
Ceci est trop long.
(sehsee eh troh lohng)

This is too short.
Ceci est trop court.
(sehsee eh troh kohrt)

This is good.
Ça va.
(sah vah)

'We seem to have a lot of novices lately.'

It fits very well.
Cela est la bonne taille.
(sehlah eh lah bohnn tahll)

Do you have a larger size?
Avez-vous une plus grande taille?
(Ahvay-vew ewn plews grahnd tahll)

Do you have a smaller size?
Avez-vous une taille plus petite?
(ahvay-vew ewn tahll plews pehteet)

Give me the next size up.
Donnez-moi la taille au-dessus.
(dohnnay-mawh lah tahll aew dehssew)

Give me the next size down.
Donnez-moi la taille en dessous.
(dohnnay-mawh lah tahll ehn dehssohew)

Do you have the same thing in another colour?
Avez-vous la même chose en une autre couleur?
(ahvay-vew lah mehm chohs ehn ewn ohtreh kohlewr)

May I try this on?
Puis-je essayer ceci?
(pew-zheh ehssayeh sehsee)

Do you have a mirror?
Avez-vous une glace?
(ahvay-vew ewn glahs)

Do you have a dressing room?
Avez-vous un salon d'essayage?
(ahvay vew ewn sahlohn dehssayahzh)

This shoe is too wide.
Cette chaussure est trop large.
(sehtt chohssewr eh troh lahrzh)

This shoe is too narrow.
Cette chaussure est trop étroite.
(sehtt chohssewr eh troh ehtrowt)

These shoes pinch my toes.
Ces chaussures me pincent les orteils.
(seh chohssewr meh peensehnt leh ohrteheel)

I like it.
Cela me plaît.
(sehlah meh plaeh)

I don't like it.
Cela ne me plaît pas.
(sehlah neh meh plaeh pah)

I'll take it.
Je le prends.
(zheh leh prehnd)

I would like a pair of ...
J'aimerais une paire de ...
(zhehahmehray ewn paer deh)

Do you sell ...?
Vendez-vous ...?
(vehnday-vew)

> golf shoes with/without spikes:
> des chaussures de golf/cloutées/non cloutées
> (deh chohssewr deh golf/klohewteh/noh klohewteh)
>
> gloves: des gants (deh gahnt)
> hats: des chapeaux (deh chahpoh)
> light jackets: des vestes légères (deh vehst lehzhehr)
> pants (trousers): des pantalons (deh pahntahlohn)
> raincoats: des imperméables (deh eempehrmehableh)
>
> shirts/short/long sleeved:
> des chemisettes/des chemises
> (deh chehmeesehtt/deh chehmees)
>
> shirts with/without a collar/pocket:
> des chemises avec/sans un col/poche
> (deh chehmees ahvehk/sahns ewn kohl/pohch)
>
> sunglasses: des lunettes de soleil (deh lewnehtt deh solay)
> sweaters: des pullovers (deh pullovers)
> t-shirts: des t-shirts (deh t-shirts)

COLOURS

beige: beige (behzh)
black: noir (nwahr)
blue: bleu (blew)
brown: brun (brahn)
cream: crème (krehm)
crimson: cramoisie (krahmoys)
gold: doré (doray)
green: vert (vehr)
grey: gris (gree)
orange: orange (orahngzh)
pink: rose (roaz)
purple: violet (vyoleh)
red: rouge (roozh)
scarlet: écarlate (aykahyrlaht)
silver: argenté (ahrzhahngtay)
turquoise: turquoise (tewrkwahz)
white: blanc (blahnk)
yellow: jaune (zhoan)

NUMBERS

0: zéro (zayroh)
1: une (ewn)
2: deux (dew)
3: trois (traw)
4: quatre (kahtr)
5: cinq (sahnk)
6: six (sees)
7: sept (seht)
8: huit (weet)
9: neuf (newf)
10: dix (dees)
11: onze (ohnz)
12: douze (dooz)
13: treize (trehz)
14: quatorze (kahtorz)
15: quinze (kahnz)
16: seize (sehz)
17: dix-sept (dees-seht)
18: dix-huit (dees-weet)

```
 19: dix-neuf (dees-newf)
 20: vingt (vang)
 21: vingt et un (vang tay ewn)
 22: vingt-deux (vangt-dew)
 23: vingt-trois (vangt-traw)
 24: vingt-quatre (vangt-kahr)
 25: vingt-cinq (vangt-sahnk)
 26: vingt-six (vangt-sees)
 27: vingt-sept (vangt-seht)
 28: vingt-huit (vangt-weet)
 29: vingt-neuf (vangt-newf)
 30: trente (trahnt)
 40: quarante (kahrahnt)
 50: cinquante (sangkahnt)
 60: soixante (swahssahnt)
 70: soixante-dix/septante (swahssahnt-dees/sehptahnt)
 80: quatre-vingts/huitante (kahtr-vangt/weetahnt)
 90: quatre-vingt-dix/nonante (kahtr-vangt-dees/nohnahnt)
100: cent (sahnt)
150: cent cinquante (sahnt sangkahnt)
200: deux cents (dew sahnt)
250: deux cents cinquante (dew sahnt sangkahnt)
300: trois cents (traw sahnt)
400: quatre cents (kahtr sahnt)
500: cinq cents (sahnk sahnt)
600: six cents (sees sahnt)
700: sept cents (seht sahnt)
800: huit cents (weet sahnt)
900: neuf cents (newf sahnt)
1,000: mille (meel)

 1st: premier (premyay)
 2nd: deuxième (dewzyehm)
 3rd: troisième (trawszyehm)
 4th: quatrième (kahtryehm)
 5th: cinquième (sahnkeeyehm)
 6th: sixième (seeseeyehm)
 7th: septième (sehteeyehm)
 8th: huitième (weeteeyehm)
 9th: neuvième (newfeeyehm)
10th: dixième (deeseeyehm)
11th: onzième (ohnzeeyehm)
12th: douzième (doozeeyehm)
```

13th: treizième (trehzeeyehm)
14th: quatorzième (kahtorzeeyehm)
15th: quinzième (kahnzeeyehm)
16th: seizième (sehzeeyehm)
17th: dix-septième (dees-sehteeyehm)
18th: dix-huitième (dees-weeteeyehm)

'Hailstones as big as golf balls can make your life difficult.'

INTERNATIONAL GOLFERS'
LANGUAGE GUIDE

ITALIAN

GUIDA LINGUISTICA DEL
GOLFISTA INTERNAZIONALE

ITALIANO

BASIC CONVERSATION

Excuse me: Mi scusi (mee skewzee)
Good morning: Buon giorno (beuon gornoh)
Good night: Buona notte (beunah notteh)
Good afternoon: Buon giorno (beuon gornoh)
Good bye: Arrivederci (arreevehderchee)
Good day: Buon giorno (beuon gornoh)
Good evening: Buona sera (beuonah serh)
Hello: ciao (chau)

I do not speak Italian.
Non parlo l'italiano.
(noh parloh leetalianoh)

I would like ...
Vorrei ...
(vorray)

I don't understand: Non capisco (noh kapeeskoh)
I understand: capisco (kapeeskoh)
No: No (noh)
Please: Per favore (pehr fahvoray)

Please bring me ...
Per favore mi porti ...
(pehr fahvoray mee portee)

Please show me ...
Per favore mi mostri ...
(pehr fahvoray mee mostree)

Please give me ...
Per favore mi dia...
(pehr fahvoray mee deeah)

See you later: A più tardi (ah pew tahrdee)
See you soon: A tra poco (a trah pokoh)
Thank you: Grazie (grahziay)
Thank you very much: Molte grazie (mohlteh grahziay)
That's alright: prego (pregoh)
Until tomorrow: A domani (ah domanee)

We would like ...
Vorremmo ...
(vorrehmmoh)

Yes: Sì (see)
Your welcome: prego (pregoh)

(questions)

Can you give me ...?
Può mi dia ...?
(pwo mee deeah)

Can I have ...?
Posso avere ...?
(possoh ahveray)

Can we have ...?
Possiamo avere ...?
(posseeamoh ahveray)

Can you show me ...?
Può mostrarmi ...?
(pwo mostrarmee)

Can you direct me to ...?
Può indicarmi la direzione per ...?
(pwo eendeekarmee lah deerezeeonay pehr)

Can you help me please?
Può aiutarmi per favore?
(pwo aewtarmee pehr fahvoray)

Can you tell me please?
Può dirmi per favore?
(pwo deermee pehr fahvoray)

Do you speak English?
Parla inglese?
(parlah eenglezee)

Do you understand?
Capisce?
(kapeeschay)

Is there anyone here who speaks English?
C'è qualcuno qui che parla inglese?
(cheh kwalkeunoh kee cheh parlah eenglezee)

Is there/are there ...?
C'è/ci sono ...?
(cheh/chee sonoh)

AT THE GOLF COURSE

No parking.
Divieto di parcheggio.
(deeveeehtoh dee parcheggeeoh)

May I park here?
Posso parcheggiare qui?
(possoh parcheggeearay kee)

Where can I park?
Dove posso parcheggiare?
(dovay possoh parcheggeearay)

Straight ahead.
Avanti diritto.
(ahvantee deereetoh)

To the right.
A destra.
(ah deestrah)

To the left.
A sinistra.
(ah seeneestrah)

Where is the nearest golf course?
Dove'è il più vicino campo di golf?
(dovay eh eel pew veesinoh kahmpoh dee golf)

Is there another golf course near here?
C'è un altro campo di golf qui vicino?
(cheh ewn ahltroh kahmpoh dee golf kee veeseenoh)

I would like some information about this course.
Vorrei qualche informazione sul campo?
(vorray keualchay informazionay seul kahmpoh)

Do you have any course information in English?
Ha particolari del campo in inglese?
(ah parteekolaree dehl kahmpoh in eenglezee)

How much is a round of golf?
Qual'è la tariffa per un giro?
(kwaleh lah tariffah pehr ewn geeroh)

How much are the green fees?
Qual'è la tassa d'ammissione?
(kwaleh lah tahssah deammissionay)

What is the fee for 9/18 holes?
Qual'è la tariffa per nove/diciotto buche?
(kwaleh lah tariffah pehr novay/deesheeottoh bewchay)

What is the rate per day/week/month?
Qual'è la tariffa giornaliera/settimantale/mensile?
(kwaleh lah tariffah gornaleerah/setteemanalay/menseelay)

Is there a discount for senior citizens?
I pensionati hanno diritto a uno sconto?
(ee penseeonatee ahnnoh deereettoh ah ewnoh skontoh)

Is there a discount for children?
I bambini hanno diritto a uno sconto?
(ee bambeenee ahnnoh deereettoh ah ewnoh skontoh)

Do I need to be a member?
Devo essere socio?
(devoh ehsseray sosheeoh)

How much is membership?
Qual'è la tassa d'iscrizione?
(kwaleh lah tassah deescreezeeonay)

Per day: Al giorno (ahl gornoh)
Per week: Alla settimana (allah setteemanah)
Per month: Al mese (ahl mayzee)
Per year: All'anno (ahll ahnnoh)

Do I need to make a reservation?
Devo fare una prenotazione?
(devoh faray ewnah prenotazeeonay)

I have a reservation.
Ho una prenotazione.
(oh ewna prenotazeeonay)

My name is ...
Mi chiamo ...
(mee cheeahmoh)

I would like to make a reservation for ...
Vorrei fare una prenotaione per ...
(vorray faray ewnah prenotazeeonay pehr)

> myself: me (may)
> ... people: ... persone (personeh)
> today: oggi (ohggee)
> this afternoon: questo pomeriggio (kewstoh pomereeggeeoh)
> this evening: stasera (staserah)
> tomorrow: domaini (domanee)
> tomorrow morning: domani mattina (domanee matteenah)
> tomorrow afternoon: domani pomeriggio (domanee pomereeggeeoh)
> tomorrow evening: domani sera (domanee serah)
> next week: la prossima settimana (la prosseemah settimanah)
>
> on: il (eel)
> Monday: lunedì (leundee)
> Tuesday: martedì (martehdee)
> Wednesday: mercoledì (mehrkoledee)
> Thursday: giovedì (geeovedee)
> Friday: venerdì (venerdee)
> Saturday: sabato (sabatoh)
> Sunday: domenica (domenikah)

at: all'/alle (ahll/alleh)
one o'clock: una (ewnah)
one thirty: una e mezzo (ewnah ee mezzoh)
two o'clock: due (deway)
two thirty: due e mezzo (deway ee mezzoh)
three o'clock: tre (treh)
three thirty: tre e mezzo (treh ee mezzoh)
four o'clock: quattro (kwattroh)
four thirty: quattro e mezzo (kwattroh ee mezzoh)
five o'clock: cinque (cheenkeway)
five thirty: cinque e mezzo (cheenkeway ee mezzoh)
six o'clock: sei (say)
six thirty: sei e mezzo (say ee mezzoh)
seven o'clock: sette (setteh)
seven thirty: sette e mezzo (setteh ee mezzoh)
eight o'clock: otto (ottoh)
eight thirty: otto e mezzo (ottoh ee mezzoh)
nine o'clock: nove (novay)
nine thirty: otto e mezzo (ottoh ee mezzoh)
ten o'clock: dieci (deechee)
ten thirty: dieci e mezzo (deechee ee mezzoh)
eleven o'clock: undieci (eundeechee)
eleven thirty: undieci e mezzo (eundeechee ee mezzoh)
twelve o'clock: dodici (dohdeechee)
twelve thirty: dodici e mezzo (dohdeechee ee mezzoh)
a.m: antimeridiane (anteemereedeeanay)
p.m: pomeridiane (pomereedeeanay)

Please write it down for me.
Me lo scriva per favore.
(may loh skrivah pehr fahvoray)

What is the dress code for the course?
Quali indumenti sono previsti per il campo di golf?
(kwalee eendumentee sonoh preveestee pehr eel kampoh dee golf)

Is there night golfing here?
Si gioca al golf di sera?
(see geeosah ahl golf dee serah)

Are U.S. Golf Association rules and regulations used here?
Si applicano le norme generali e il regolamento dell 'associazione
  golfistica americana?
(see appleekanoh leh normeh generalee e eel regolamentoh
  dellahssosiazionay golfeestikah amerikanah)

Do you accept tee off times?
Si accettano ore d'inizio?
(see aksettanoh oray deeneezeeoh)

At what time does the course open/close?
A che ora si apre/si chiude il campo?
(ah cheh ohrah see ahpray/see cheuday eel kahmpoh)

Is there a club house here?
Il campo ha una sede del circolo?
(eel kampoh ah ewnah sedeh dehl sirkohoh)

At what time does the club house open/close?
A che ora si apre/si chiude la sese del circolo?
(ah chay orah see apray/see cheeuday lah seseh dehl sirkoloh)

Is there a pro-shop here?
Il campo ha un negozio di articoli da golf?
(eel kampoh ah ewn negozeeoh dee arteekolee dah golf)

At what time does the pro-shop open/close?
A che ora si apre/si chiude il negozio con l'annesso ufficio?
(ah chay orah see apray/see cheeuday eel negozeeoh kon
  lannessoh ewfeeseeoh)

Do you need to be a member to use the club house/pro-shop?
Occore essere socio per avere accesso alla sede del circolo/al
  neozio con l'annesso ufficio?
(ossoray ehssehray sosheeoh pehr ahvehray ahssehssoh ahllah
  sehdeh dehl seerkoloh/ahl negozeeoh kohn lannessoh
  ewfeeseeoh)

Is there a putting green/chipping green/driving range?
Esistono piazzole d'allenamento per tiri brevi/per tiri con ostacoli/
  terreni d'allenamento per tiri lunghi?
(ehseestono peeahzzolay dahllenahmenthoh pehr teeree brehvee/
  pehr teeree kohn ohstahkolee/tehrreenee dahllenahmentoh
  pehr teeree lewngee)

Is there a practice green?
C'è una piazzola d'allenamento?
(cheh ewnah peeahzzolah dahllenahmentoh)

Can I get a caddie here?
Posso procurarmi sul luogo un portamazze?
(possoh prokeurarmee seul leuogoh ewn portahmahzzay)

What is the going rate for a caddie?
Qual'è la tariffa corrente di un portamazze?
(kwaleh lah tahreefah korrenteh dee ewn portahmahzzay)

Do you have a map of the course?
Ha una pianta del campo?
(ah ewnah peeantah dehl kahmpoh)

Where is hole ... located?
Dove si trova la buca ...?
(dovay see trovah lah bookah)

Can you show me where the ... is located?
Può indicarmi la posizione del ...?
(pwo eendeekarmee lah poseezeeonay dehl)

> golf club: circolo golfistico (seerkoloh golfeestikoh)
> club house: sede del circolo (sedeh dehl seerkoloh)
> pro-shop: negozio di articoli da golf (negozeeoh dee arteekolee dah golf)

Are spiked shoes required at this course?
Questo campo richiede scarpe chiodate?
(kwestoh kahmpoh reecheeday skarpay cheeodatay)

How long is the course?
Qual'è la lunghezza del campo?
(kwahleh lah lewnghezzah dehl kahmpoh)

9 hole: a nove buche (ah novay bewchay)
18 hole: a diciotto buche (ah deecheeottoh bewchay)

What is the length of this hole?
Qual'è la distanza tra la piazzola di partenza e questa buca?
(kwahleh lah deestanzah trah lah peeazzolah dee partenzah ee kwestah bookah)

What is par for this hole?
Quanti tiri sono necessari tra la piazzola di partenza e questa buca?
(kwantee teeree sonoh nehsehssaree trah lah peeazzolah dee partenzah ee kwestah bookah)

Is there a residential professional at this course?
Il campo dispone di un professionale residente?
(eel kahmpoh deesponay dee ewn professionalay rehseedentay)

What does he/she charge per ½ hour/hour?
Qual'è la sua tariffa per mezz'ora/un'ora?
(kwahleh lah seuah tareeffah pehr mezzohrah/ewnohrah)

PAYING

I would like to pay for ... green fees for ... round(s)/all day.
Vorrei pagare la tariffa per ... piazzole/per ... giro(giri)/per l'intera giornata.
(vorray pagaray lah tareeffah pehr ... peeazzolay/pehr ... geeroh(geeree)/pehr leenterah geeornatah)

Must I pay in advance?
Devo pagare in anticipo?
(devoh pagaray een anteeseepoh)

May I pay in advance?
Posso pagare in anticipo?
(possoh pagaray een anteeseepoh)

Must I pay cash?
Devo pagare in contanti?
(devoh pagaray een kontantee)

May I pay by personal cheque?
Posso pagare con assegno bancario?
(possoh pagaray kohn assegnoh bankareeoh)

May I pay with traveller cheques?
Posso pagare con assegno turistico?
(possoh pagaray kohn assegnoh tewreesteekoh)

May I pay by credit card?
Posso pagare con carta di credito?
(possoh pagaray kohn kartah dee krehdeetoh)

Do you accept ...?
Si accettano carte di credito ...?
(see aksehttahnoh kartah dee krehdetoh ...)

What will the total cost be?
Qual'è sarà la spesa totale?
(kwahleh sahrah lah spehsah tohtahlay)

What is the total cost?
Qual'è la spesa totale?
(kwahleh lah spehsah tohtahlay)

We would like to pay separately.
Vorremmo pagare separatamente.
(vohrrehmmoh pahgahray sehparahtahmehntay)

I only have large bills.
Ho soltanto banconote di grosso taglio.
(oh sohltahntoh bahnkohnohtay dee grohssoh tahgleeoh)

Do you have any change?
Può cambiarmi?
(pwo kahmbeeahrmee)

I would like some small change.
Vorrei un po' di spiccioli.
(vorray ewn poh dee speekkeeolee)

Who do I make the cheque out to?
A che devo rilasciare l'assegno.
(ah chay dehvoh reelahskeeahray lahssehgnoh)

Here is my identification.
Ecco un documento d'identità.
(ehchoh ewn dokewmehntoh dee aidehnteetah)

bank card: carta bancaria (kartah bahnkahreeah)
driving licence: patente di guide (pahtehntay dee geedah)
passport: passaporto (pahssahpohrtoh)

May I have a receipt?
Può rilasciarmi una ricevuta?
(pwo reelahscheeahrmee ewnah reesehvewtah)

RENTING

I would like to rent ...
Vorrei affittare ...
(vorray ahffeettahray)

We would like to rent ...
Vorremmo affittare ...
(vorraymmoh ahffeettahray)

How much is it to rent (a) ...?
Qual'è la tariffa d'affitto per (un/una) ...
(kwahleh lah tahreeffah dahffeettoh pehr (ewn/ewnah)

Where can I rent a/a pair of ...?
Dove posso affittare un paio di/un/una ...
(dohvay pohssoh ahffeettahreh ewn paheeoh dee/ewn/ewna)

> for ½ hour: per mezz'ora (pehr mehzzohrah)
> for an hour: per un'ora (pehr ewn ohra)
> for a day: per la giornata (pehr lah geeohrnahtah)

GOLF EQUIPMENT

ball marker(s): disco(dischi) segnapalla (deeskoh(deeschee)
  sehgnahpahllah)
box of golf balls: scatola di palle da golf (skahtolah dee pahlleh
  dah golf)
divot repair tool: arnese riparazione zolle (ahrnehsay
  reepahrahzohnay zohlleh)
golf bag: sacca per mazze da golf (sahkkah pehr mahzzay dah
  golf)
golf bag umbrella: ombrellone della sacca da golf (ohmbrehllonay
  dehllah sohkkah dah golf)
golf balls: palle da golf (pahlleh dah golf)
golf car: vettura per campo di golf (vehttewrah pehr kahmpoh
  dee golf)

golf cart: carrello per campo di golf (kahrrehlloh pehr kahmpoh dee golf)

golf clubs: mazze da golf (mahzzay dah golf)

golf club cover: coprimazza (kohpreemahzzah)

iron: mazza con spatola in ferro (mahzzah kohn spahtohlah een fehrroh)

long iron: mazza con spatola in ferro per lunghe distanze (mahzzah kohn spahtohlah een fehrroh pehr lewngee deestanzay)

middle iron: mazza con spatola in ferro per distanze medie (mahzzah kohn spahtohlah een fehrroh pehr deestanzay mehdee)

pin: asta della bandiera (ahstah dehllah hahndeerah)

pitching wedge: mazza angolare per lancio (mahzzah ahngohlahray pehr lahnseeoh)

putter: putter/mazza (putter/mahzzah)

rake: rastrello (rahstrehlloh)

sand wedge: mazza angolare da bunker (mahzzah ahngohlahray dah bunker)

score card: segnapunto (sehgnahpewntoh)

shoe spike(s): chiodo da scarpa (cheeohdoh dah skahrpah)

shoe spike tool: arnese per chiodi da scarpa (ahrnehsay pehr checohdee dah skahrpah)

short iron: mazza con spatola in ferro per distance corto (mahzzah kohn spahtohlah een fehrroh pehr deestanzay kohrtoh)

tee(s): tee

wedge: mazza angolare per lancio (mahzzah ahngohlahray pehr lahnseeoh)

wood: mazza con spatola in bosco (mahzzah kohn spahtohlah een bohskoh)

wood cover(s): copri per mazza di bosco (kohpree pehr mahzzah dee bohskoh)

wood sock(s): copri per mazza di bosco (kohpree pehr mahzzah dee bohskoh)

CLUBS

1 wood: mazza di bosco numero uno (mahzzah dee bohskoh newmehroh ewnoh)

2 wood: mazza di bosco numero due (mahzzah dee bohskoh newmehroh deway)

3 wood: mazza di bosco numero tre (mahzzah dee bohskoh newmehroh treh)

4 wood: mazza di bosco numero quattro (mahzzah dee bohskoh newmehroh kwattroh)

5 wood: mazza di bosco numero cinque (mahzzah dee bohskoh newmehroh cheenkeway)

6 wood: mazza di bosco numero sei (mahzzah dee bohskoh newmehroh say)

7 wood: mazza di bosco numero sette (mahzzah dee bohskoh newmehroh setteh)

8 wood: mazza di bosco numero otto (mahzzah dee bohskoh newmehroh ottoh)

9 wood: mazza di bosco numero nove (mahzzah dee bohskoh newmehroh novay)

1 iron: mazza di ferro numero uno (mahzzah dee fehrroh newmehroh ewnoh)

2 iron: mazza di ferro numero due (mahzzah dee fehrroh newmehroh deway)

3 iron: mazza di ferro numero tre (mahzzah dee fehrroh newmehroh treh)

4 iron: mazza di ferro numero quattro (mahzzah dee fehrroh newmehroh kwattroh)

5 iron: mazza di ferro numero cinque (mahzzah dee fehrroh newmehroh cheenkeway)

6 iron: mazza di ferro numero sei (mahzzah dee fehrroh newmehroh say)

7 iron: mazza di ferro numero sette (mahzzah dee fehrroh newmehroh setteh)

8 iron: mazza di ferro numero otto (mahzzah dee fehrroh newmehroh ottoh)

9 iron: mazza di ferro numero nove (mahzzah dee fehrroh newmehroh novay)

GOLF TERMS

slice: colpo che taglia la palla (kohlpoh chay tahgleeah lah pahllah)

hook: tiro a gancio (teeroh ah gahncheeoh)

Mulligan: tipo di mazza (teepoh dee mahzzah)

handicap: handicap (handikap)

double bogey: due colpi in eccesso alla norma (deway kohlpee
   een eksehssoh ahllah nohrmah)
bogey: un colpo in eccesso alla norma (ewn kohlpoh een
   eksehssoh ahllah nohrmah)
par: norma (nohrmah)
birdie: un colpo al di sotto della norma (ewn kohlpoh ahl dee
   sohttoh dehllah nohrmah)
eagle: aquila (ahkeelah)
double eagle: tre colpi al di sotto della norma (treh kohlpee ahl
   dee sohttoh dehllah nohrmah)

AT THE PRO-SHOP

I am just looking.
Do solo un'occhiata.
(doh sohloh ewn oksheeahtah)

I would like to buy ...
Vorrei comprare ...
(vorray kohmprahray)

What size is this?
Che misura è questo?
(cheh meesewrah eh kewehstoh)

What size is that?
Che misura è quello?
(cheh meesewrah eh kewehlloh)

What size are these?
Che misura sono questi?
(che meesewrah sohno kewehstee)

I would like size ...
Vorrei la misura ...
(vorray lah meesewrah)

I wear size ...
Porto la misura ...
(pohrtoh lah meesewrah)

extra large: massima (mahsseemah)
large: grande (grahnday)
medium: media (mehdeeah)
small: piccola (peekkohlah)
extra small: minima (meeneemah)
long: lunga (lewngah)
short: corta (kohrtah)
regular: regulare (rehgewlahray)

This is too large.
E' troppo grande.
(ay trohppoh grahnday)

This is too small.
E' troppo piccola.
(ay trohppoh peekkohlah)

This is too long.
E' troppo lunga.
(ay trohppoh lewngah)

This is too short.
E' troppo corta.
(ay trohppoh kohrtah)

This is good.
Questo va bene.
(kewehstoh vah behnay)

It fits very well.
Va alla perfezione.
(vah ahllah pehrfehzeeohnay)

Do you have a larger size?
Ha una misura superiore?
(ah ewnah meesewrah sewpehreeohray)

Do you have a smaller size?
Ha una misura inferiore?
(ah ewnah meesewrah eenfehreeohray)

Give me the next size up.
Mi dia la misura immediatamente superiore.
(mee deeah lah meesewrah eemmeedeeahtahmehntay
  sewpeereeohray)

Give me the next size down.
Mi dia la misura immediatamente inferiore.
(me deeah lah meesewrah eemmeedeeahtahmehntay
  eenfehreeohray)

Do you have the same thing in another colour?
Ha lo stesso articolo in una tinta diversa?
(ah loh stehssoh ahrteekohloh een ewnah teentah deevehrsah)

May I try this on?
Posso provarlo?
(pohssoh prohvahrloh)

Do you have a mirror?
Ha un specchio?
(ah ewnoh spehscheeoh)

Do you have a dressing room?
Ha uno spogliatoio?
(ah ewnoh spohgleeahtoheeoh)

This shoe is too wide.
Questa scarpa è troppo larga.
(kwehstah skahrpah eh trohppoh lahrgah)

This shoe is too narrow.
Questa scarpa è troppo stretta.
(kwehstah skahrpah eh trohppoh strehttah)

These shoes pinch my toes.
Queste scarpe mi stringono le dita.
(kwehsteh skahrpeh mee streengohnoh leh deetah)

I like it.
Mi piace.
(mee peeahsay)

I don't like it.
Non mi piace.
(nohn mee peeahsay)

I'll take it.
lo/la prendo.
(loh/lah prehndoh)

I would like a pair of ...
Vorrei un paio di ...
(vorray ewn paheeoh dee)

Do you sell ...?
Vende ...?
(vehnday)

> golf shoes with/without spikes:
> scarpe da golf/chiodate/non chiodate
> (skahrpeh dah golf/cheeohdahtay/nohn cheeohdahtay)
>
> gloves: guanti (gewahntee)
> hats: cappelli (kahppehllee)
> light jackets: giacchette (geeahschehttay)
> pants (trousers): pantaloni/calzoni (pahntahlohnee/
>   kahlzohnee)
> raincoats: impermeabile (eempehrmehahbeelay)
>
> shirts/short/long sleeved:
> camicia/corte/maniche lunghe
> (kahmeeseeah/kohrtay/mahneechay lewnghay)
>
> shirts with/without a collar/pocket:
> camicia con/non colletto/taschino
> (kahmeeseeah kohn/nohn kohllehttoh/tahscheenoh)
>
> sunglasses: occhiali da sole (ohscheeahlee dah sohlay)
> sweaters: maglione (mahgleeohnay)
> t-shirts: maglietta (mahgleehttah)

COLOURS

beige: beige (baizh)
black: nero (nayroh)
blue: blu (blew)
brown: marrone (mahrronay)
cream: crema (krehmah)
crimson: cremisi (krehmeesee)
gold: dorato (dohrahtoh)
green: verde (vehrday)
grey: grigio (greejoh)
orange: arancio (ahrahnchoh)
pink: rosa (rohsah)
purple: viola (veeolah)
red: scarlatto (skahrlahttoh)
scarlet: turchese (tewrkayzay)
silver: argentato (ahrgehntahtoh)
turquoise: turchese (tewrkayzay)
white: bianco (beeahnkoh)
yellow: giallo (gahlloh)

NUMBERS

0: zero (zehroh)
1: uno (ewnoh)
2: due (deway)
3: tre (treh)
4: quattro (kwattroh)
5: cinque (cheenkeway)
6: sei (say)
7: sette (setteh)
8: otto (ottoh)
9: nove (novay)
10: dieci (deehchee)
11: undici (ewndeechee)
12: dodici (dohdeechee)
13: tredici (trehdeechee)
14: quattordici (kwattrohdeechee)
15: quindici (keweendeechee)
16: sedici (saydeechee)
17: diciassette (deecheesetteh)
18: diciotto (deecheeottoh)

19: diciannove (deecheenovay)
20: venti (vayntee)
21: ventuno (vayntewnoh)
22: ventdue (vayntdeway)
23: ventitre (vaynteetrehay)
24: ventiquattro (vaynteekwattroh)
25: venticinque (vaynteecheenkeway)
26: ventisei (vaynteesay)
27: ventisette (vaynteesetteh)
28: ventotto (vayntottoh)
29: ventinove (vaynteenovay)
30: trenta (trehntah)
40: quaranta (kewahrahntah)
50: cinquanta (cheenkewntah)
60: sessanta (sehssahntah)
70: settanta (sehttahntah)
80: ottanta (ottahntah)
90: novanta (nohvahntah)
100: cento (chehntoh)
150: centocinquanta (chehntohcheenkewntah)
200: duecento (dewaychehntoh)
250: duecentocinquanta (dewaychehntohcheenkewntah)
300: trecento (trehchehntoh)
400: quattrocento (kwattrohchehntoh)
500: cinquecento (cheenkewaychehntoh)
600: seicento (saychehntoh)
700: settecento (settehchehntoh)
800: ottocento (ottohchehntoh)
900: novecento (novaychehntoh)
1,000: mille (meelay)

1st: primo (preemoh)
2nd: secondo (sehkohndoh)
3rd: terzo (tehrzoh)
4th: quarto (kwahrtoh)
5th: quinto (keweentoh)
6th: sesto (sehstoh)
7th: settimo (sehtteemoh)
8th: ottavo (ottahvoh)
9th: nono (nohnoh)
10th: decimo (dehcheemoh)
11th: undicesimo (ewndeechehseemoh)
12th: dodicesimo (dohdeechehseemoh)

13th: tredicesimo (trehdeechehseemh)
14th: quattordicesimo (kwahttohrdeehehseemoh)
15th: quindicesimo (keweendeechehseemoh)
16th: sedicesimo (sehdeechehseemoh)
17th: diciassettesimo (deecheeahssettehseemoh)
18th: diciottesimo (deecheeottehseemoh)

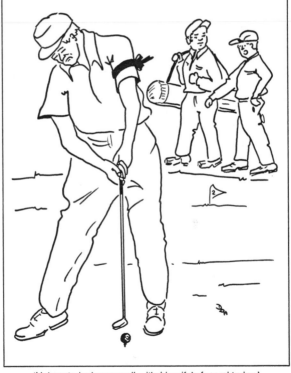

'He's not playing so well – it's his wife's funeral today.'

INTERNATIONAL GOLFERS' LANGUAGE GUIDE

SPANISH

GUÍA INTERNACIONAL DEL LENGUAJE DEL GOLF

ESPAÑOL

'I've kept the sermon short so that you good people can get out and enjoy the spring sunshine.'

BASIC CONVERSATION

Excuse me: Perdóneme (pehrdohnehmay)
Good morning: Buenos días (bewnos deeahs)
Good night: Buenas noches (bewnahs nochays)
Good afternoon: Buenas tardes (bewnahs tahrdays)
Good bye: Adiós (ahdeeohs)
Good day: Buenos días (bewnos deeahs)
Good evening: Buenas tardes (bewnahs tahrdays)
Hello: Hola (ohlah)

I do not speak Spanish.
No hablo español.
(noh ahbloh ehspahnohl)

I would like ...
Quisiera ...
(keeseehrah)

I don't understand: No comprendo (noh kompreendoh)
I understand: Comprendo (kompreendoh)
No: No (noh)
Please: Por favor (pohr fahvohr)

Please bring me ...
Por favor tráigame ...
(pahr fahvohr trahgahmay)

Please show me ...
Por favor enséñeme ...
(pohr fahvohr ehnsehnehmay)

Please give me ...
Por favor deme ...
(pohr fahvohr daymay)

See you later: Hasta luego (ahstah looaygoh)
See you soon: Hasta luego (ahstah looaygoh)
Thank you: Gracias (grahseeahs)
Thank you very much: Muchas gracias (moochahs grahseeahs)
That's alright: Está bien (ehstah beeyen)
Until tomorrow: Hasta mañana (ahstah manyahnah)

We would like ...
Quisiéramos ...
(keeseehrahmos)

Yes: Sí (see)
Your welcome: De nada (day nahdah)

(questions)

Can you give me ...?
¿Puede deme?
(pewdeh daymay)

Can I have ...?
¿Puede darme?
(pewdeh dahrmay)

Can we have ...?
¿Puede darnos ...?
(pewdeh dahrnohs)

Can you show me ...?
¿Puede usted enseñarme?
(pewdeh ewstehd ehnsehnahrmay)

Can you direct me to ...?
¿Puede usted indicarme la dirección a ...?
(pewdeh ewstehd eendeekahrmay lah deerehkseeyon ah)

Can you help me please?
¿Puede usted ayudarme, por favor?
(pewdeh ewstehd ahewdahrmay, pohr fahvohr)

Can you tell me please?
¿Puede usted decirme, por favor?
(pewdeh ewstehd dehseermay, pohr fahvohr)

Do you speak English?
¿Habla usted inglés?
(ahblah ewstehd eenglays)

Do you understand?
¿Comprende usted?
(kohmpreenday ewstehd)

Is there anyone here who speaks English?
¿Hay alguien aquí que hable inglés?
(ai ahlgewn ahkee kay ahbleh eenglays)

Is there/are there ...?
¿Hay/ hay ...?
(ai/ai)

AT THE GOLF COURSE

No parking.
Prohibido el aparcamiento.
(proheebeedoh ehl ahparkahmeentoh)

May I park here?
¿Se puede aparcar aquí?
(see pewdeh ahpahrkahr ahkee)

Where can I park?
¿Dónde se puede aparcar?
(dohnday see pewdeh ahpahrkahr)

Straight ahead.
Enfrente.
(ehnfrehntay)

To the right.
A la derecha.
(ah lah dehraychah)

To the left.
A la izquierda.
(ah lah eezkewehrdah)

Where is the nearest golf course?
¿Donde está el campo de golf más próximo?
(dohnday ehstah ehl kahmpoh deh golf mahs prohkseemoh)

Is there another golf course near here?
¿Hay otro campo de golf cerca de aquí?
(ai ohtroh kahmpoh deh golf serkah deh ahkee)

I would like some information about this course.
Me gustaría información sobre este campo.
(may gewstahreeah informaseeyon sohbray ehsteh kahmpoh)

Do you have any course information in English?
¿Tienen ustedes información en inglés sobre el campo?
(teehnehn ewstehdehs informasiyon ehn eenglays sohbray ehl
    kahmpoh)

How much is a round of golf?
¿Cuánto cuesta una partida de golf?
(kwahntoh kewstah oonah pahrteedah deh golf)

How much are the green fees?
¿Cuánto es la tarifa del césped?
(kwahntoh ehs lah tahreefah dehl sehspehd)

What is the fee for 9/18 holes?
¿Cuál es la tarifa por una ronda de nueve hoyos/dieciocho hoyos?
(kwahl ehs lah tahreefah pohr oonah rohndah deh nooehvay
    oyohs/deeseeohohoh oyohs)

What is the rate per day/week/month?
¿Cual es la tarifa por día/semana/mes?
(kwahl ehs lah tahreefah pohr deeah/seemahnah/mays)

Is there a discount for senior citizens?
¿Hay descuento para jubilados?
(ai dehskewntoh pahrah hewbeelahdohs)

Is there a discount for children?
¿Hay descuento para los niños?
(ai dehskewntoh pahrah lohs neenyohs)

Do I need to be a member?
¿Se necesita ser socio?
(see nehsehseetah sehr sohseeoh)

How much is membership?
¿Cuánto cuesta la afiliación?
(kwahntoh kwehstah lah ahfeeleeahseeyon)

Per day: Por día (pohr deeah)
Per week: Por semana (pohr seemahnah)
Per month: Por mes (pohr mays)
Per year: Por año (pohr ahnyoh)

Do I need to make a reservation?
¿Se necesita reservar?
(see nehseeseetah rehsehrvahr)

I have a reservation.
Tengo una reservación.
(teengoh oonah reeseervaseeyon)

My name is ...
Me llamo ...
(may yahmoh)

I would like to make a reservation for ...
Me gustaría tener una reservación para ...
(may gewstahreeah tehnehr oonah rehsehrvaseeyon pahrah)

> myself: mí (mee)
> ... people: ... personas (pehrsohnahs)
> today: hoy (oy)
> this afternoon: este tarde (ehsteh tahrday)
> this evening: esta noche (ehstah nohchay)
> tomorrow: mañana (manyahnah)
> tomorrow morning: mañana por la mañana (manyahnah pohr lah manyahnah)
> tomorrow afternoon: mañana por la tarde (manyahnah pohr lah tahrday)
> tomorrow evening: mañana por la noche (manyahnah pohr lah nohchay)
> next week: la semana que viene (lah seemahnah kay veenay)
>
> on: el día (ehl deeah)
> Monday: lunes (lewnays)
> Tuesday: martes (mahrtays)

Wednesday: miércoles (meerkolays)
Thursday: jueves (hewvays)
Friday: viernes (veernays)
Saturday: sábado (sahbahdoh)
Sunday: domingo (dohmeengoh)

at: para (pahrah)
one o'clock: la una (lah oonah)
one thirty: la una y media (lah oonah ee mehdeeah)
two o'clock: las dos (lahs dohs)
two thirty: las dos y media (lahs dohs ee mehdeeah)
three o'clock: las tres (lahs trays)
three thirty: las tres y media (lahs trays ee mehdeeah)
four o'clock: las cuatro (lahs kwahtroh)
four thirty: las cuatro y media (lahs kwahtroh ee mehdeeah)
five o'clock: las cinco (lahs seenkoh)
five thirty: las cinco y media (lahs seenkoh ee mehdeeah)
six o'clock: las seis (lahs says)
six thirty: las seis y media (lahs says ee mehdeeah)
seven o'clock: las siete (lahs seehtay)
seven thirty: las siete y media (lahs seehtey ee mehdeeah)
eight o'clock: las ocho (lahs ohchoh)
eight thirty: las ocho y media (lahs ohchoh ee mehdeeah)
nine o'clock: las nueve (lahs nooehvay)
nine thirty: las nueve y media (lahs nooehvay ee mehdeeah)
ten o'clock: las diez (lahs deehs)
ten thirty: las diez y media (lahs deehs ee mehdeeah)
eleven o'clock: las once (lahs ohnsay)
eleven thirty: las once y media (lahs ohnsay ee mehdeeah)
twelve o'clock: las doce (lahs dohsay)
twelve thirty: las doce y media (lahs dohsay ee mehdeeah)
a.m: de la mañana (dee lah manyahnah)
p.m: de la noche (dee lah nohchay)

Please write it down for me.
Por favor, póngalo por escrito.
(pohr fahvohr, pohngahloh pohr ehskreetoh)

What is the dress code for the course?
¿Cómo debe uno vestirse para este campo de golf?
(kohmoh daybay oonoh vehsteersay pahrah ehsteh kahmpoh deh golf)

Is there night golfing here?
¿Se juega golf de noche aquí?
(see hewaygah golf deh nohchay ahkee)

Are U.S. Golf Association rules and regulations used here?
¿Se utilizan las normas y reglamento de la Asociación de Golf de
    Estados Unidos aquí?
(see ewteeleezahn lahs nohrmahs ee rehglahmehntoh deh lah
    assoseeaseeyon deh golf deh ehstahdos ewneedohs ahkee)

Do you accept tee off times?
¿Aceptan ustedes horas de inicio?
(asehptahn ewstehdehs ohrahs deh eeneeseeoh)

At what time does the course open/close?
¿A qué hora se abre/cierra el campo de golf?
(ah kay ohrah see ahbray/seehrrah ehl kahmpoh deh golf)

Is there a club house here?
¿Hay algún pabellón del club aquí?
(ai ahlgoon pahbehlyohn dehl clewb ahkee)

At what time does the club house open/close?
¿A qué hora se abre/cierra el pabellón?
(ah kay ohrah see ahbray/seehrrah ehl pahbehlyohn)

Is there a pro-shop here?
¿Hay alguna tienda de artícuos de golf?
(ai ahlgoonah teehndah deh ahrteekewlohs deh golf)

At what time does the pro-shop open/close?
¿A qué hora abre/cierra la tienda de artículos de golf?
(ah kay ohrah ahbray/seehrrah lah teehndah deh ahrteekewlohs
    deh golf)

Do you need to be a member to use the club house/pro-shop?
¿Es necesario ser socio para utilizar el pabellón/la tienda de golf?
(ehs nehsehsahreeoh sehr sohseeoh pahrah ewteeleezahr ehl
    pahbehlyohn/lah teendah deh golf)

Is there a putting green/chipping green/driving range?
¿Hay algún césped de prácticas de jugada/alcance de rodada?
(ai ahlgoon sehspehd deh prahkteekhs deh hewgahdah/
    ahlkahnsay deh rohdahdah)

Is there a practice green?
¿Hay algún cesped de prácticas?
(ai ahlgoon sehspehd deh prahkteekahs)

Can I get a caddie here?
¿Se puede conseguir un cadi aquí?
(see pewdeh konsehgewr oon kadee ahkee)

What is the going rate for a caddie?
¿Cuál es la tarifa actual por un cadi?
(kwahl ehs lah tahreefah ahktewahl pohr oon kadee)

Do you have a map of the course?
¿Tienen un mapa del campo?
(teehnehn oon mahpah dehl kahmpoh)

Where is hole ... located?
¿Dónde se encuentra el hoyo ...?
(dohnday see ehnkewntrah ehl oyoh)

Can you show me where the ... is located?
¿Puede mostrarme dónde se encuentra el ...?
(pewdeh mohstrahrmay dohnday see ehnkewntrah ehl)

> golf club: club de golf (clewb deh golf)
> club house: pabellón del club (pahbehlyohn dehl club)
> pro-shop: tienda de artículos de golf (tehndah deh
> ahrteekewlohs deh golf)

Are spiked shoes required at this course?
¿Se requieren zapatos con púas en este campos?
(see reekewehrehn zahpahtohs kohn pewahs ehn ehsteh
kahmpoh)

How long is the course?
¿Qué longitud tiene el campo de golf?
(kay lohngeetewd teeneh ehl kahmpoh deh golf)

9 hole: nueve hoyos (nooehvay oyohs)
18 hole: dieciocho hoyos (deeseeeohchoh oyohs)

What is the length of this hole?
¿Cual es la longitud de este hoyo?
(kwahl ehs lah lohngeetewd deh ehsteh oyoh)

What is par for this hole?
¿Qué número de tiradas para este hoyo?
(kay newmehroh deh teerahdahs pahrah ehsteh oyoh)

Is there a residential professional at this course?
¿Hay algún profesional residente en este campo de golf?
(ai ahlgoon prohfehseeonahl rehseedehnteh ehn ehsteh kahmpoh
    deh golf)

What does he/she charge per ½ hour/hour?
¿Cuánto carga por media/una hora?
(kwahntoh kahrgah pohr mehdeeah/oonah ohrah)

PAYING

I would like to pay for ... green fees for ... round(s)/all day.
Deseo pagar la tarifa de cesped/por ... partida(s)/por todo el dia.
(dehsehoh pahgahr lah tahreefah deh sehspehd/pohr...
    pahrteedah(s)/pohr tohdoh ehl deeah)

Must I pay in advance?
¿Debe pagarse por anticipado?
(daybeh pahgahrsay pohr ahnteeseepahdoh)

May I pay in advance?
¿Puedo pagar por anticipado?
(pewdoh pahgahr pohr ahnteeseepahdoh)

Must I pay cash?
¿Debo pagar en efectivo?
(dayboh pahgahr ehn ehfehkteevoh)

May I pay by personal cheque?
¿Puedo pagar con un cheque personal?
(pewdoh pahgahr kohn oon chehkay pehrsohnahl)

May I pay with traveller cheques?
¿Puedo pagar con un cheque de viajero?
(pewdoh pahgahr kohn oon chehkay deh veeahehroh)

May I pay by credit card?
¿Puedo pagar con tarjeta de crédito
(pewdoh pahgahr kohn tahrhehtah deh krehdeetoh)

Do you accept ...?
¿Acepta la tarjeta ...?
(aksehptah lah tahrhehta ...)

What will the total cost be?
¿Cuánto será el coste total?
(kwahntoh sehrah ehl kohsteh tohtahl)

What is the total cost?
¿Cuánto es el coste total?
(kwahntoh ehs ehl kohsteh tohtahl)

We would like to pay separately.
Quisieramos pagar por separdo.
(keeseehrahmohs pahgahr pohr sehpahrahdoh)

I only have large bills.
Solamente tengo billetes grandes.
(sohlahmehntay teengoh beelyehtehs grahndays)

Do you have any change?
¿Tiene cambio?
(teehnay kahmbeeoh)

I would like some small change.
Me gustaría cambios pequeños.
(may gewstahreeah kahmbeeos pehkeenyohs)

Who do I make the cheque out to?
¿A quién extiendo este cheque?
(ah keeyehn ehksteehndoh ehsteh chehkay)

Here is my identification.
Aquí tiene mi identificación.
(ahkee teehnay mee aidehnteefeekaseeyohn)

bank card: tarjeta bancaria (tahrhehtah bahnkahreeah)
driving licence: permiso de conducir (pehrmeesoh deh kohndewseer)
passport: pasaporte (pahsahpohrtay)

May I have a receipt?
¿Me puede dar un recibo?
(may pewdeh dahr oon rehseeboh)

RENTING

I would like to rent ...
Quisiera alquilar ...
(keeseehrah ahlkeelahr)

We would like to rent ...
Quiséramos alquilar ...
(keeseehrahmohs ahlkeelahr)

How much is it to rent (a) ...?
¿Cuánto cuesta alquilar (un/a) ...?
(kwahntoh kewhstah ahlkeelahr (oon/ah))

Where can I rent a/a pair of ...?
¿Dónde puedo alquilar un/ par de ...?
(dohnday pewdoh ahlkeelahr oon/ pahr deh)

> for ½ hour: para media hora (pahrah mehdeeah hohrah)
> for an hour: para una hora (pahrah oonah hohrah)
> for a day: para un dia (pahrah oon deeah)

GOLF EQUIPMENT

ball marker(s): marcador(es) de bolas (mahrkahdohr(ehs) deh bohlahs)
box of golf balls: una caja de bolas de golf (oonah kahah deh bohlahs deh golf)
divot repair tool: herramienta para reparar el césped (ehrrahmeehntah pahra reepahrahr ehl sehspehd)
golf bag: bolsa de golf (bohlsah deh golf)
golf bag umbrella: paraguas de golf (pahragewahs deh golf)
golf balls: bolas de golf (bohlahs deh golf)
golf car: carro de golf (kahrroh deh golf)
golf cart: carretilla de golf (kahrrehteeyah deh golf)
golf clubs: palos de golf (pahlohs deh golf)

golf club cover: cubierta para palo de golf (kewbeehrtah pahrah pahloh deh golf)

iron: palo de hierro (pahloh deh eehrroh)

long iron: palo de distancia (pahloh deh deestahnseeah)

middle iron: palo intermedio (pahloh eentehrmehdeeoh)

pin: banderín (bahndehreen)

pitching wedge: cuña (kewnyah)

putter: putter (putter)

rake: rastrillo (rahstreeyoh)

sand wedge: cuña para bunker (kewnyah pahrah bunker)

score card: tarjeta/tanteador (tahrhehtah/tahntehahdohr)

shoe spike(s): clavo(s) para zapatos (klahvoh(s) pahrah zahpahtohs)

shoe spike tool: herramienta para los clavos para zapatos (ehrrahmeehntah pahrah lohs klahvohs pahrah zahpahtohs)

short iron: palo corto (pahloh kohrtoh)

tee(s): tee(s) (tee(s))

wedge: wedge (wehdj)

wood: palo de madera (pahloh deh mahdehrah)

wood cover(s): cubierta para palo de madera (kewbeehrtah pahrah pahloh deh mahdehrah)

wood sock(s): cubierta para palo de madera (kewbeehrtah pahrah pahloh deh mahdehrah)

CLUBS

1 wood: palo de madera numero uno (pahloh deh mahdehrah newmehroh oonoh)

2 wood: palo de madera numero dos (pahloh deh mahdehrah newmehroh dohs)

3 wood: palo de madera numero tres (pahloh deh mahdehrah newmehroh trays)

4 wood: palo de madera numero cuatro (pahloh deh mahdehrah newmehroh kwahtroh)

5 wood: palo de madera numero cinco (pahloh deh mahdehrah newmehroh seenkoh)

6 wood: palo de madera numero seis (pahloh deh mahdehrah newmehroh says)

7 wood: palo de madera numero siete (pahloh deh mahdehrah newmehroh seehtay)

8 wood: palo de madera numero ocho (pahloh deh mahdehrah newmehroh ohchoh)

9 wood: palo de madera numero nueve (pahloh deh mahdehrah newmehroh nooehvay)

1 iron: palo de hierro numero uno (pahloh deh eehrroh newmehroh oonoh)

2 iron: palo de hierro numero dos (pahloh deh eehrroh newmehroh dohs)

3 iron: palo de hierro numero tres (pahloh deh eehrroh newmehroh trays)

4 iron: palo de hierro numero cuatro (pahloh deh eehrroh newmehroh kwahtroh)

5 iron: palo de hierro numero cinco (pahloh deh eehrroh newmehroh seenkoh)

6 iron: palo de hierro numero seis (pahloh deh eehrroh newmehroh says)

7 iron: palo de hierro numero siete (pahloh deh eehrroh newmehroh seehtay)

8 iron: palo de hierro numero ocho (pahloh deh eehrroh newmehroh ohchoh)

9 iron: palo de hierro numero nueve (pahloh deh eehrroh newmehroh nooehvay)

GOLF TERMS

slice: corte (kohrtay)
hook: enganche (ehngahnchay)
Mulligan: mulligan (mulligan)
handicap: handicap (handikap)
double bogey: bogey doble (bohgee dohblay)
bogie: bogey (bohgee)
par: par (pahr)
birdie: birdie (birdee)
eagle: eagle/águila (eegel/ahgeelah)
double eagle: eagle doble/águila doble (eegel dohblay/ahgeelah dohblay)

AT THE PRO-SHOP

I am just looking.
Solamente estoy mirando.
(sohlohmehntay ehstoy meerahndoh)

I would like to buy ...
Quisiera comprar ...
(keeseehrah kohmprahr)

What size is this?
¿Qué tamaño es esto?
(kay tahmahnyoh ehs ehstoh)

What size is that?
¿Qué tamaño es eso?
(kay tahmanyoh ehs ehsoh)

What size are these?
¿Qué tamaño son estos?
(kay tahmahnyoh sohn ehstohs)

I would like size ...
Me gustaría el tamaño ...
(may gewstahreeah ehl
  tahmahnyoh)

'You've got to appreciate what the
wild life people do for us – but this is
ridiculous!'

I wear size ...
Tomo el tamaño ...
(tohmoh ehl tahmahnyoh)

> extra large: muy grande (mooee grahnday)
> large: grande (grahnday)
> medium: medio (meedeeoh)
> small: pequeño (pehkehnyoh)
> extra small: muy pequeño (mooee pehkehnyoh)
> long: largo (lahrgoh)
> short: corto (kohrtoh)
> regular: regular (raygewlahr)

This is too large.
Esto es demasiado grande.
(ehstoh ehs deemahseeahdoh grahnday)

This is too small.
Esto es demasiado pequeño.
(ehstoh ehs deemahseeahdoh pehkehnyoh)

This is too long.
Esto es demasiado largo.
(ehstoh ehs deemahseeahdoh lahrgoh)

This is too short.
Esto es demasiado corto.
(ehstoh ehs deemahseeahdoh kohrtoh)

This is good.
Esto está bien.
(ehstoh ehstah beehn)

It fits very well.
Me sienta muy bien/me va muy bien.
(may seehntah mooee beehn/may vah mooee beehn)

Do you have a larger size?
¿Tiene un tamaño más grande?
(teehnay oon tahmahnyoh mahs grahnday)

Do you have a smaller size?
¿Tiene un tamaño más pequeño?
(teehnay oon tahmahnyoh mahs pehkehnyoh)

Give me the next size up.
Déme el tamaño siguiente más grande.
(daymay ehl tahmahnyoh seegewehntay mahs grahnday)

Give me the next size down.
Déme el tamaño siguiente más pequeño.
(daymay ehl tahmahnyoh seegewehntay mahs pehkehnyoh)

Do you have the same thing in another colour?
¿Tiene lo mismo, pero en otro color?
(teenay loh meesmoh, pehroh ehn ohtroh kohlohr)

May I try this on?
¿Puedo probar esto?
(pewehdoh prohbahr ehstoh)

Do you have a mirror?
¿Tiene un espejo?
(teehnay oon ehspayhoh)

Do you have a dressing room?
¿Tiene un vestuario?
(teehnay oon vehstooahreeoh)

This shoe is too wide.
Este zapato es demasiado ancho.
(ehsteh zahpahtoh ehs deemahseeahdoh ahnchoh)

This shoe is too narrow.
Este zapato es demasiado estrecho.
(ehsteh zahpahtoh ehs deemahseeahdoh ehstrehchoh)

These shoes pinch my toes.
Estos zapatos me aprietan.
(ehstohs zahpahtohs may ahpreehtahn)

I like it.
Me gusta.
(may gewstah)

I don't like it.
No me gusta.
(noh may gewstah)

I'll take it.
Lo tomaré.
(loh tohmahray)

I would like a pair of ...
Me gustaria un par de ...
(may gewstahreeah oon pahr deh)

Do you sell ...?
¿Vende ...?
(vehnday)

    golf shoes with/without spikes:
    zapatos de golf con/sin púas
    (zahpahtohs deh golf kohn/seen pewahs)

    gloves: guantes (gewahntays)
    hats: sombreros (sohmbrehrohs)
    light jackets: chaquetas ligeras (jahkehtays leegehrahs)

pants (trousers): pantalones (pahntahlohnays)
raincoats: impermeable (eempehrmehahblay)

shirts/short/long sleeved:
camisa/corta/de manga larga
(kahmeesah/kohrtah/deh mahngah lahrgah)

shirts with/without a collar/pocket:
camisa con/sin cuello/bolsillo
(kahmeesah kohn/seen kewehlyoh/bohlseeyoh)

sunglasses: gafas de sol/anteojos de sol (gahfahs dee sohl/
ahnteeohhos dee sohl)
sweaters: suéter (sooehtehr)
t-shirts: camiseta (kahmeesehtah)

COLOURS

beige: beige (behzh)
black: negro (naygroh)
blue: azul (ahzewl)
brown: marrón (mahrrohn)
cream: crema (kraymah)
crimson: carmesí (kahrmehsee)
gold: oro (ohroh)
green: verde (vehrday)
grey: gris (grees)
orange: naranja (nahrahnhah)
pink: rosa (rohsah)
purple: purpúreo (pewrpewrehoh)
red: rojo (rohoh)
scarlet: escarlata (ehskahrlahtah)
silver: plata (plahtah)
turquoise: turquesa (tewrkehsah)
white: blanco (blahnkoh)
yellow: amarillo (ahmahreeyoh)

'The way he's going he'll soon be
playing the Australian open.'

NUMBERS

0: cero (sehroh)
1: uno (oonoh)
2: dos (dohs)
3: tres (trays)
4: cuatro (kwahtroh)
5: cinco (seenkoh)
6: seis (says)
7: siete (seehtay)
8: ocho (ohchoh)
9: nueve (nooehvay)
10: diez (deehs)
11: once (ohnsay)
12: doce (dohsay)
13: trece (traysay)
14: catorce (kahtohrsay)
15: quince (keensay)
16: dieciséis (deeseesays)
17: diecisiete (deeseeseehtay)
18: dieciocho (deeseeohchoh)
19: diecinueve (deeseenooehvay)
20: veinte (behntay)
21: veintiuno (behntayoonoh)
22: veintidós (behntaydohs)
23: veintitrés (behntaytrays)
24: veinticuatro (behntaykwahtroh)
25: veinticinco (behntayseenkoh)
26: veintiséis (behntaysays)
27: veintisiete (behntayseehtay)
28: veintiocho (behntayohchoh)
29: veintinueve (behntaynooehvay)
30: treinta (trehntah)
40: cuarenta (kwahrehntah)
50: cincuenta (seenkwehntah)
60: sesenta (sehsehntah)
70: setenta (sehtehntah)
80: ochenta (ohchehntah)
90: noventa (nohvehntah)
100: cien (seehn)
150: ciento cincuenta (seehntoh seenkwehntah)
200: doscientos (dohsseehntohs)
250: doscientos cincuenta (dohsseehntohs seenkwehntah)

```
  300: trescientos  (traysseehentohs)
  400: cuatrocientos  (kwatrohseehntohs)
  500: quinientos  (keeneehntohs)
  600: seiscientos  (saysseehntohs)
  700: setecientos  (sehtehseehntohs)
  800: ochocientos  (ohchohseehntohs)
  900: novecientos  (nohvayseehntohs)
1,000: mil  (meel)
```

```
  1st: primero  (preemehroh)
  2nd: segundo  (saygewndoh)
  3rd: tercero  (tehsehroh)
  4th: cuarto  (kwahrtoh)
  5th: quinto  (keentoh)
  6th: sexto  (sehkstoh)
  7th: séptimo  (sehpteemoh)
  8th: octavo  (ahktahvoh)
  9th: noveno  (nohvehnoh)
 10th: décimo  (dayseemoh)
 11th: undécimo  (ewndayseemoh)
 12th: duodécimo  (dewohdayseemoh)
 13th: decimotercio  (dayseemohtehrseeoh)
 14th: decimocuarto  (dayseemohkwahrtoh)
 15th: decimoquinto  (dayseemohkeentoh)
 16th: decimosexto  (dayseemohsehkstoh)
 17th: decimoséptimo  (dayseemohsehpteemoh)
 18th: decimooctavo  (dayseemohahktahvoh)
```

'I did warn you son to keep away from that
driving range.'

INTERNATIONAL GOLFERS'
LANGUAGE GUIDE

PORTUGUESE

GUIA INTERNACIONAL DE
LINGUA PARA GOLFISTA

PORTUGÊS

'Sorry, you'll have to take the "down" escalator. Our records show
you lied about your handicap.'

BASIC CONVERSATION

Excuse me: Perdão (pehrdahaew)
Good morning: Bom dia (bohm deeah)
Good night: Boa noite (bohah nohtay)
Good afternoon: Boa tarde (bohah tahrday)
Good bye: Adeus (ahdeeoosh)
Good day: Bom dia (bohm deeah)
Good evening: Boa noite (bohah nohtay)
Hello: Olá (ohlah)

I do not speak Poruguese.
Não falo portugês
(nahaew fahloh phrtewgesh)

I would like ...
Queria ...
(kehreeah)

I don't understand: Não compreendo (nahaew kohmprehndoh)
I understand: Compreendo (kohmprehndoh)
No: Não (nahaew)
Please: Por favor (pohr fahvohr)

Please bring me ...
Por favor traga-me ...
(pohr fahvohr trahgah may)

Please show me ...
Por favor mostre-me ...
(pohr fahvohr mohstray may)

Please give me ...
Por favor dê-me ...
(pohr fahvohr day-may)

See you later: Até logo (ahtay lohgoh)
See you soon: Até logo (ahtay lohgoh)
Thank you: Obrigado (ohbreegahdoh)
Thank you very much: Muito obrigado (meweetoh ohbreegahdoh)
That's alright: Não tem de quê (nahaew taym deh kay)
Until tomorrow: Até amanhã (ahtay ahmahnah)

We would like ...
Queríamos ...
(kehreeahmosh)

Yes: Sim (seem)
Your welcome: De nada (day nahdah)

(questions)

Can you give me ...?
Pode dê-me ...?
(pohdeh day-may)

Can I have ...?
Pode dar-me ...?
(pohdeh dahr-may)

Can we have ...?
Pode dar-nos ...?
(pohdeh dahr-nohsh)

Can you show me ...?
Pode mostrar-me ...?
(pohdeh mohstrahr-may)

Can you direct me to ...?
Pode indicar-me a direcção para ...?
(pohdeh eendeekahr may ah deerehksahaew pahrah)

Can you help me please?
Pode ajudar-me por favor ?
(pohdeh ahewdahr may pohr fahvohr)

Can you tell me please?
Pode dizer-me por favor ...?
(pohdeh deezehr may pohr fahvohr)

Do you speak English?
Fala inglês?
(fahlah eenglaysh)

Do you understand?
Compreende?
(kohmprehenday)

Is there anyone here who speaks English?
Há aqui alguém que fale inglês?
(ah ahkee ahlgooehm kay fahleh eenglaysh)

Is there/are there ...?
Há?/há ...?
(ah/ah)

AT THE GOLF COURSE

No parking.
Estacionamento proibido.
(ehstahseeohnamehntoh proheebeedoh)

May I park here?
Pode-se estacionar aqui?
(pohdeh-say ehstahseeohnahr ahkee)

Where can I park?
Onde se pode estacionar?
(ohnday say pohdeh ehstahseeohnahr)

Straight ahead.
Sempre em frente.
(sehmpray ehm frehntay)

To the right.
á direita.
(ah deerehtah)

To the left.
á esquerda.
(ah ehskewehrdah)

Where is the nearest golf course?
Onde é o campo de golfe mais próximo?
(ohnday ay oh kahmpoh deh golf mais prohkseemoh)

Is there another golf course near here?
Há outro campo de golfe perto daqui?
(ah ohewtroh kahmpoh deh golf pehrtoh dahkee)

I would like some information about this course.
Gostaria de ter alguma informação sobre este campo?
(gohstahreeah deh tehr ahlgoomah eenfohrmahsaew sohbray
    ehsteh kahmpoh)

Do you have any course information in English?
Tem alguma informação em inglês sobre o campo?
(taym ahlgoomah eenfohrmahsaew ehm eenglaysh oh kahmpoh)

How much is a round of golf?
Quanto custa uma partida de golfe?
(kwahntoh kewstah oomah pahrteedah deh golf)

How much are the green fees?
Quanto é a tarifa do relvado?
(kwahntoh ay ah tahreefah doh rehlvahdoh)

What is the fee for 9/18 holes?
Qual é a tarifa para nove buracos/dezoito buracos?
(kwahl ay ah tahreefah pahrah nohveh bewrahkohsh/dezahoytoh
    boorahkohsh)

What is the rate per day/week/month?
Qual é a tarifa por dia/semana/mês?
(kwahl ay ah tahreefah pohr deeah/sehmahnah/maysh)

Is there a discount for senior citizens?
Há desconto para terceira idade?
(ah dehskohntoh pahrah tehrsayrah eedahday)

Is there a discount for children?
Há desconto para crianças?
(ah dehskohntoh pahrah kreeahnsahs)

Do I need to be a member?
É preciso ser sócio?
(ay prehseesoh sehr sohseeoh)

How much is membership?
Quanto custa a inscrição?
(kwahntoh kewstah ah eenskreesaew)

Per day: por dia (pohr deeah)
Per week: por semana (pohr sehmahnah)
Per month: por mês (pohr maysh)
Per year: por ano (pohr ahnoh)

Do I need to make a reservation?
É preciso reservar?
(ay prehseesoh rehsehrvahr)

I have a reservation.
Fiz uma reserva.
(feesh oomah rehsehrvah)

My name is ...
O meu nome é ...
(oh mehew nohmay ay)

I would like to make a reservation for ...
Gostava de fazer uma reserva para ...
(gohstahvah deh fahzehr oomah rehsehrvah pahrah)

> myself: mim (meem)
> ... people: ... pessoas (pehssohahs)
> today: hoje (ohyay)
> this afternoon: esta tarde (ehstah tahrday)
> this evening: esta noite (ehstah nohtay)
> tomorrow: amanhã (ahmahnah)
> tomorrow morning: amanhã de manhã (ahmahnah deh
>   mahnah)
> tomorrow afternoon: amanhã à tarde (ahmahnah ah
>   tahrday)
> tomorrow evening: amanhã à noite (ahmahnah ah nohtay)
> next week: a próxima semana (ah prohkseemah
>   sehmahnah)
>
> on: na (nah)
> Monday: segunda-feira (saygewndah fehrah)
> Tuesday: terça-feira (tehrsah fehrah)
> Wednesday: cuarta-feira (kwahrtah fehrah)

Thursday: quinta-feira (keentah fehrah)
Friday: sexta-feira (sehkstah fehrah)
Saturday: sábado (sahbahdoh)
Sunday: domingo (dohmeengoh)

at: à (ah)
one o'clock: uma hora (oomah ohrah)
one thirty: uma e meia (oomah eh meheeah)
two o'clock: duas horas (dewahsh ohrash)
two thirty: duas e meia (dewahsh eh meheeah)
three o'clock: três horas (traysh ohrash)
three thirty: três e meia (traysh eh meheeah)
four o'clock: quatro horas (kwahtroh ohrash)
four thirty: quatro e meia (kwahtroh eh meheeah)
five o'clock: cinco horas (seenkoh ohrash)
five thirty: cinco e meia (seenkoh eh meheeah)
six o'clock: seis horas (saysh ohrash)
six thirty: seis e meia (saysh eh meheeah)
seven o'clock: sete horas (sehteh ohrash)
seven thirty: sete e meia (sehteh eh meheeah)
eight o'clock: oito horas (oytoh ohrash)
eight thirty: oito e meia (oytoh eh meheeah)
nine o'clock: nove horas (nohveh ohrash)
nine thirty: nove e meia (nohveh eh meheeah)
ten o'clock: dez horas (dehsh ohrash)
ten thirty: dez e meia (dehsh eh meheeah)
eleven o'clock: onze horas (ohnzeh ohrash)
eleven thirty: onze e meia (ohnzeh eh meheeah)
twelve o'clock: meio dia (meheeoh deeah)
twelve thirty: meio dia e meia hora (meheeoh deeah eh
    meheeah ohrah)
a.m: da manhã (dah mahnah)
p.m: da tarde (dah tahrday)

Please write it down for me.
Escreva isso para mim, por favor.
(ehskreevah eessoh pahrah meem, pohr fahvohr)

What is the dress code for the course?
Qual é o código para o compo?
(kwahl ay oh kohdeegoh pahrah oh kahmpoh)

Is there night golfing here?
Aqui há golfe nocturno?
(ahkee ah golf nahktewrnoh)

Are U.S. Golf Association rules and regulations used here?
As normas e regulamentos da associação de golfe dos estados
    unidos são usados aqui?
(ash nohrmash eh rehgewlahmehntosh dah ahssohseeashaew deh
    golf dosh ehshtahdosh ewneedosh saew ewshahdosh ahkee)

Do you accept tee off times?
Aceitam horas de abertura?
(ahsaytahm ohrash deh ahbehrtewrah)

At what time does the course open/close?
A que horas abre/fecha o campo?
(ah kay ohrash ahbray/fehchah oh kahmpoh)

Is there a club house here?
Há aqui algum pavilhão do clube?
(ah ahkee ahlgoom pahveelaew doh klewb)

At what time does the club house open/close?
A que horas abre/fecha o pavilhão?
(ah kay ohrash ahbray/fehchah oh pahveelaew)

Is there a pro-shop here?
Há aqui alguma loja de artigos de golfe?
(ah ahkee ahlgooma lohah deh ahrteegosh deh golf)

At what time does the pro-shop open/close?
A que horas abre/fecha a loja de artigos de golfe?
(ah kay ohrash ahbray/fehchah ah lohah deh ahrteegosh deh golf)

Do you need to be a member to use the club house/pro-shop?
É necessário ser sócio para usar o pavilhão/a loja de artigos de
    golfe?
(ay nehsehsahreeoh sehr sohseeoh pahrah ewsahr oh
    pahveelaew/ah lohah deh ahrteegosh deh golf)

Is there a putting green/chipping green/driving range?
Há algum relvado para praticar jogadas/a distÂncia de condução?
(ah ahlgoom rehlvahdoh pahrah prahteekahr hohgahdash/ah
    deestahnseeah deh kohndewsaew)

Is there a practice green?
Há algum relvado para praticar?
(ah ahlgoom rehlvahdoh pahrah prahteekahr)

Can I get a caddie here?
Posso arranujar um cadi aqui?
(pohssoh ahrrahnewhahr oom kadee ahkee)

What is the going rate for a caddie?
Qual é a tarifa actual para um cadi?
(kwahl ay ah tahreefah ahtewahl pahrah oom kadee)

Do you have a map of the course?
Tem um mapa do campo?
(taym oom mahpah doh kahmpoh)

Where is hole ... located?
Onde fica o buraco número ...
(ohnday feechah oh boorahkoh newmehroh)

Can you show me where the ... is located?
Pode mostrar-me onde fica ...?
(pohdeh mohshtrahr may ohnday feechah)

> golf club: o clube de golfe (oh klewb deh golf)
> club house: o pavilhão do clube (oh pahveelaew doh klewb)
> pro-shop: a loja de artigos de golfe (ah lohah deh ahrteegosh deh golf)

Are spiked shoes required at this course?
É preciso sapatos de pregos para este campo?
(ay prehseeshoh sahpahtohsh deh prehgosh pahrah ehsteh kahmpoh)

How long is the course?
Que comprimento tem o campo?
(kay kohmpreemehntoh taym oh kahmpoh)

9 hole: nove buracos (nohveh boorahkosh)
18 hole: dezoito buracos (dezahoytoh boorahkosh)

What is the length of this hole?
Qual é a distância deste buraco?
(kwahl ay ah deestahnseeah dehshteh boorahkoh)

What is par for this hole?
Qual é o número de tacadas para este buraco?
(kwahl ay oh newmehroh deh tahahdash pahrah ehsteh
   boorahkoh)

Is there a residential professional at this course?
Há algum profissional residente neste campo de golfe?
(ah ahlgoom prohfeesseeohnahl rehseedehntay nehstay kahmpoh
   deh golf)

What does he/she charge per ½ hour/hour?
Quanto leva ele/ela por meia hora/uma hora?
(kwahntoh lehvah ehl/ehlah pohr meheeah ohrah/oomah ohrah)

PAYING

I would like to pay for ... green fees for ... round(s)/all day.
Queria pagar a tarifa de relvado para ... partida(s)/por odo o dia.
(keehrah pahgahr ah tahreefah deh rehlvahdoh
   pahrah...pahrteeda(sh)/pohr ohdoh oh deeah)

Must I pay in advance?
Devo pagar adiantado?
(dehvoh pahgahr ahdeeahtahdoh)

May I pay in advance?
Posso pagar adiantado?
(pohssoh pahgahr ahdeeahntahdoh)

Must I pay cash?
Devo pagar em dinheiro?
(dehvoh pahgahr ehm deenehroh)

May I pay by personal cheque?
Posso pagar com cheque?
(pohssoh pahgahr kohm chehkay)

May I pay with traveller cheques?
Posso pagar com cheque de viagem?
(pohssoh pahgahr kohm chehkay deh veeahgehm)

May I pay by credit card?
Posso pagar com cartão de crédito?
(pohssoh pahgahr kohm kahrtaew deh krehdeetoh)

Do you accept ...?
Aceitam o cartão ...?
(ahsaytahm oh kahrtaew ...)

What will the total cost be?
Quanto sera o custo total?
(kwahntoh sehrah oh kewstoh tohtahl)

What is the total cost?
Quanto é o custo total?
(kwahntoh ay oh kewstoh tohtahl)

We would like to pay separately.
Queríamos pagar em separado?
(kehreeahmosh pahgahr ehm sehpahrahdoh)

I only have large bills.
Só tenho notas grades.
(soh tehnoh nohtash grandaysh)

Do you have any change?
Tem troco?
(taym trohkoh)

I would like some small change.
Gostava de alguns trocados.
(gohstahvah deh ahlgoonash trohkahdosh)

Who do I make the cheque out to?
A quem passo o cheque?
(ah kewehm pahssoh oh chehkay)

Here is my identification.
Aqui está a minha identificação.
(ahkee ehstah ah meenah aidehnteefeekasaew)

bank card: cartão do banco (kahtaew doh bahnkoh)
driving licence: licença de condução (leesehsah deh kohndewsaew)
passport: passporte (passpohrtay)

May I have a receipt?
Pode dar-me um recibo?
(pohdeh dahr may oom rehseeboh)

RENTING

I would like to rent ...
Queria alugar ...
(kehreeah ahlewgahr)

We would like to rent ...
Queríamos alugar ...
(kehreeahmosh ahlewgahr)

How much is it to rent (a) ...?
Quanto custa alugar (um/a)
(kwahntoh kewstah ahlewgahr (oom/ah)

Where can I rent a/a pair of ...?
Onde posso alugar um/um par de...?
(ohnday pohssoh ahlewgahr oom/oom pahr deh)

>   for ½ hour: por meia hora (pohr meheeah ohrah)
>   for an hour: por uma hora (pohr oomah ohrah)
>   for a day: por um dia (pohr oom deeah)

GOLF EQUIPMENT

ball marker(s): marcador(es) de bola (mahrkahdohr(ehsh) deh bohlah)
box of golf balls: caixa de bolas de golfe (kaihah deh bohlash deh golf)
divot repair tool: forqueta para reparação de relvado (fohkehtah pahrah reepahrahsaew deh rehlvahdoh)
golf bag: saco de golfe (sahkoh deh golf)
golf bag umbrella: guarda-sol de golfe (gewahrdah sohl deh golf)

golf balls: bolas de golfe (bohlash deh golf)
golf car: carro de golfe (kahrroh deh golf)
golf cart: cart de golfe (kahrt deh golf)
golf clubs: tacos de golfe (tahkosh deh golf)
golf club cover: saco de tacos de golfe (sahkoh deh tahkosh deh golf)
iron: ferro (fehrroh)
long iron: ferro longo (fehrroh lohngoh)
middle iron: ferro medio (fehrroh mehdeeoh)
pin: bandeira (bahndehrah)
pitching wedge: taco de pitching (tahkoh deh pitching)
putter: putter (putter)
rake: ancinho (ahnseenoh)
sand wedge: taco para areia (tahkoh deh ahreeah)
score card: cartão(s) de pontução (kahrtaew(sh) deh pohntewsaew)
shoe spike(s): prego(s) de sapato (praygoh(sh) deh sahpahtoh)
shoe spike tool: forqueta para pregos de sapato (fohrkehtah pahrah praygosh deh sahpahtoh)
short iron: ferro curto (fehrroh kewrtoh)
tee(s): tee(s) (tee(sh))
wedge: wedge (wehdj)
wood: madeira (mahdehrah)
wood cover(s): coberta(s) de tacos de madeira (kohbehtah(sh) deh tahkohsh deh mahdehrah)
wood sock(s): coberta(s) de tacos de madeira (kohbehtah(sh) deh tahkohsh deh mahdehrah)

CLUBS

1 wood: madeira número uma (mahdehrah newmehroh oomah)
2 wood: madeira número dois (mahdehrah newmeroh doysh)
3 wood: madeira número três (mahdehrah newmehroh traysh)
4 wood: madeira número quatro (mahdehrah newmehroh kwahtroh)
5 wood: madeira número cinco (mahdehrah newmehroh seenkoh)
6 wood: madeira número seis (mahdehrah newmehroh saysh)
7 wood: madeira número sete (mahdehrah newmehroh sehteh)
8 wood: madeira número oito (mahdehrah newmehroh oytoh)
9 wood: madeira número nove (mahdehrah newmehroh nohveh)

1 iron: ferro número um (fehrroh newmehroh oom)
2 iron: ferro número dois (fehrroh newmehroh doysh)
3 iron: ferro número três (fehrroh newmehroh traysh)
4 iron: ferro número quatro (fehrroh newmehroh kwahtroh)
5 iron: ferro número cinco (fehrroh newmehroh seenkoh)
6 iron: ferro número seis (fehrroh newmehroh saysh)
7 iron: ferro número sete (fehrroh newmehroh sehteh)
8 iron: ferro número oito (fehrroh newmehroh oytoh)
9 iron: ferro número nove (fehrroh newmehroh noveh)

GOLF TERMS

slice: slice (slais)
hook: hook (hook)
Mulligan: Mulligan (mulligan)
handicap: handicap (handikap)
double bogey: double bogey (dewbehl bohgee)
bogey: bogey (bohgee)
par: par (pahr)
birdie: birdie (birdee)
eagle: eagle (eegel)
double eagle: double eagle (dewbehl eegel)

AT THE PRO-SHOP

I am just looking.
Só estou a ver.
(soh ehshtoew ah vehr)

I would like to buy ...
Queria comprar.
(kehreeah kohmprahr)

What size is this?
Que tamanho é este?
(kay tahmahnoh ay ehsteh)

What size is that?
Que tamanho é aquele?
(kay tahmahnoh ay ahkewleh)

'It's either that or a divorce.'

What size are these?
Que tamanho são estes?
(kay tahmahnoh saew ehstehsh)

I would like size ...
Gostaria do tamanho ...
(gohstahreeah doh tahmahnoh)

I wear size ...
Eu visto/calço tamanho ...
(ehew veestoh/kahlsoh tahmahnoh)

> extra large: extra grande (ehkstrah grahnday)
> large: grande (grahnday)
> medium: médio (mehdeeoh)
> small: pequeno (perkaynoh)
> extra small: extra pequeno (ehkstrah perkaynoh)
> long: comprido (kohmpreedoh)
> short: curto (kewrtoh)
> regular: regular (rehgewlahr)

This is too large.
Este é muito grande.
(ehsteh ay meweetoh grahnday)

This is too small.
Este é muito pequeno.
(ehsteh ay meweetoh perkaynoh)

This is too long.
Este é muito comprido.
(ehsteh ay meweetoh kohmpreedoh)

This is too short.
Este é muito curto.
(ehsteh ay meweetoh kewrtoh)

This is good.
Este está bom.
(ehsteh ehstah bohm)

It fits very well.
Este assenta muito bem.
(ehsteh ahssehntah meweetoh behm)

Do you have a larger size?
Tem um tamanho maior?
(taym oom tahmahnoh maiohr)

Do you have a smaller size?
Tem um tamanho mais pequeno?
(taym oom tahmahnoh maheesh perkaynoh)

Give me the next size up.
De-mê o tamanho acima.
(day may oh tahmahnoh ahseemah)

Give me the next size down.
Dê-me o tamanho abaixo.
(day may oh tahmahnoh abaihoh)

Do you have the same thing in another colour?
Tem o mesmo noutra cor?
(taym oh mehshmoh nohewtrah kohr)

May I try this on?
Posso provar este?
(pohssoh prohvahr ehsteh)

Do you have a mirror?
Tem um espelho?
(taym oom ehspehloh)

Do you have a dressing room?
Tem um gabinete de provas?
(taym oom gahbeenehtay deh prohvahsh)

This shoe is too wide.
Este sapato está muito largo.
(ehsteh sahpahtoh ehstah lahrgah)

This shoe is too narrow.
Este sapato está muito apertado.
(ehsteh sahpahtoh ehstah meweetoh ahpehrtahdoh)

These shoes pinch my toes.
Estes sapatos magoam-me os dedos.
(ehstehsh sahpahtosh mahgohahm may ohsh dehdohsh)

I like it.
Gosto deste.
(gohstoh dehstay)

I don't like it.
Não gosto deste.
(nahaew gohstoh dehstay)

I'll take it.
Eu levo isso.
(ehew lehvoh eessoh)

I would like a pair of ...
Queria um par de ...
(kehreeah oom pahr deh)

Do you sell ...?
Vende ...?
(vehnday)

'It's not odd – you forgot the club is sponsored by the Alcoholics Anonymous.'

golf shoes with/without spikes:
Sapatos de golfe com/sem pregos
(sahpahtosh deh golf kohm/sehm prehgosh)

gloves: luvas (lewvash)
hats: chapéus (shahpewsh)
light jackets: casacos leves (kahsahsohsh lehvehsh)
pants (trousers): calças (kahlsash)
raincoats: gabardine (gahbahrdeeneh)

shirts/short/long sleeved:
camisa/curta/de manga comprida
(kahmeesah/kewrtah/deh mahngah kohmpreedah)

shirts with/without a collar/pocket:
Camisa com/sem colarinho/bolso
(kahmeesah kohm/sehm kohlahreenoh/bohlsoh)

sunglasses: óculos de sol (ohkewlohsh deh sohl)

sweaters: camisola (kahmeesohlah)
t-shirts: camiseta (kahmeesehtah)

COLOURS

beige: bege (behzh)
black: preto (praytoh)
blue: azul (ehrzewl)
brown: castanho/marrom (kahstahnyooh/mahrrohm)
cream: creme (krehm)
crimson: carmesim (kahrmehseem)
gold: dourado (dohrahdoh)
green: verde (vayrdeh)
grey: cinzento (seenzayntoh)
orange: cor de laranja (kohr deh lahrahnyah)
pink: cor de rosa (kohr deh rohsah)
purple: roxo (rohshoh)
red: vermelho (vehrmaylyoh)
scarlet: escarlate (ehskahrlahtay)
silver: prateado (prahtyahdoh)
turquoise: azul-turquesa (ehrzewl-tewrkehsah)
white: branco (brahnkoh)
yellow: amarelo (ehrmahrehloh)

NUMBERS

0: zero (zehroh)
1: um (oom)
2: dois (doysh)
3: três (traysh)
4: quatro (kwahtroh)
5: cinco (seenkoh)
6: seis (saysh)
7: sete (sehteh)
8: oito (oytoh)
9: nove (nohveh)
10: dez (dehsh)
11: onze (ohnzeh)
12: doze (dohzeh)
13: treze (trayzeh)
14: catorze (kahtohrzeh)

15: quinze (keenzeh)
16: dezasseis (dezahsaysh)
17: dezassete (dezahsehteh)
18: dezoito (dezahoytoh)
19: dezanove (dezahnohveh)
20: vinte (veenteh)
21: vinte e um (veenteh eh oom)
22: vinte e dois (veenteh eh doysh)
23: vinte e três (veenteh eh traysh)
24: vinte e quatro (veenteh eh kwahtroh)
25: vinte e cinco (veenteh eh seenkoh)
26: vinte e seis (veenteh eh saysh)
27: vinte e sete (veenteh eh sehteh)
28: vinte e oito (veenteh eh oytoh)
29: vinte e nove (veenteh eh nohveh)
30: trinta (treentah)
40: quarenta (kwahrehntah)
50: cinquenta (seenkwehntah)
60: sessenta (sehssehntah)
70: setenta (sehtehntah)
80: oitenta (oytehntah)
90: noventa (nohvehntah)
100: cem/cento (sehm/sehmtoh)
150: cento e cinquenta (sehmtoh eh seenkwehntah)
200: duzentos (doozayntosh)
250: duzentos e cinquenta (doozayntosh eh seenkwehntah)
300: trezentos (trayzehntosh)
400: quatrocentos (kwahtrohsehntosh)
500: quinhentos (keweenehntosh)
600: seiscentos (sayshsehntosh)
700: setecentos (sehtehsehntosh)
800: oitocentos (oytohsehntosh)
900: novecentos (nohvehsehntosh)
1,000: mil (meel)

1st: primeiro (preemayroh)
2nd: segundo (sehgewndoh)
3rd: terceiro (tehrsayroh)
4th: quarto (kwahrtoh)
5th: quinto (keentoh)
6th: sexto (sayshtoh)
7th: sétimo (sehteemmoh)
8th: oitavo (oytahvoh)

9th: nono (nohnoh)
10th: décimo (dehseemmoh)
11th: undécimo (ewndehseemmoh)
12th: duodécimo (dewohdehseemmoh)
13th: decimotercio (dehseemohtehrseoh)
14th: decimoquarto (dehseemohkwahrtoh)
15th: decimoquinto (dehseemohkeentoh)
16th: decimosexto (dehseemohsayshtoh)
17th: decimosétimo (dehseemohsehteemmoh)
18th: decimooitavo (dehseemohoytahvoh)

NOTES

NOTES

NOTES

AVAILABLE SOON IN THIS SERIES

Do you speak Doctor?
A comprehensive multi-lingual medical phrase book.

- Latin American version (English-Spanish/Spanish-English)

- Western European Version I (English-Spanish-Portuguese-French-Italian)

- Western European Version II (English-Dutch-German)

- Scandinavian Version (English-Norwegian-Danish-Swedish-Finnish)

- Asian Version I (English-Mandarin-Cantonese-Japanese-Korean)

- Asian Version II (English-Thai-Malay-Indonesian-Vietnamese)

- Indian Version (English-Hindi-Punjabi-Urdu-Bengali)

- African Version (English-Portuguese-French-Swahili-Afrikaans)

Do you speak car repair?
A comprehensive multi-lingual phrase book concerning the car

- Western European version (10 languages)

Do you speak night club?
A comprehensive multi-lingual phrase book intended to help you in the night club scene while vacationing abroad.

- Western European version (10 languages)

- Asian Version (10 languages)

AN AUTOGRAPHED COPY OF THIS BOOK?

If you would like an autographed copy for yourself or that special golfer please send $4.95 (Canada/Australia $5.95, U.K. £2.95) plus $1.25 (Canada/Australia $2.25, U.K. £1.50) for postage and handling and this form to:

Pandemic International Publishers Inc.
POB 61849
Vancouver, Washington 98666
(USA)

Mr. Mrs. Miss _____

Address: _____

City _____ State (country) _____ Zip(post code) _____

Please rush me _____ autographed copies of "Do you speak golf".

Enclosed is my check/money order for

(Please allow 3 weeks for shipment.)